The Game

The Game Planners

Transforming Canada's Sport System

DONALD MACINTOSH
and
DAVID WHITSON

McGill-Queen's University Press
Montreal & Kingston • London • Buffalo

© McGill-Queen's University Press 1990
ISBN 0-7735-0758-2 (cloth)
ISBN 0-7735-1211-X (paper)

Legal deposit second quarter 1990
Bibliothèque nationale du Québec

Printed in Canada on acid-free paper
First paperback edition 1994

This book was first published with the help of a grant
from the Social Science Federation of Canada, using
funds provided by the Social Sciences and Humanities
Research Council of Canada.

Canadian Cataloguing in Publication Data
Macintosh, Donald
    The game planners

Includes bibliographical references.
ISBN 0-7735-0758-2 (bound) –
ISBN 0-7735-1211-X (pbk.)

1. Sports and state – Canada. I. Whitson, David,
1945–   . II. Title.
GV585.M26 1990   306.4'83'0971   C90-090030-X

This book was set in 10/12 Souvenir (Bitstream) by
Q Composition Inc.

Contents

Tables

Acknowledgments

The study of sport policy making in selected national sport organizations that provided the empirical data for this book was supported by a grant from the Social Sciences and Humanities Research Council of Canada. We are grateful for this support. Both the School of Graduate Studies and Research and the Faculty of Arts and Science at Queen's University provided financial assistance for the final preparation of the manuscript. We also wish to acknowledge the work of the other persons involved in this original study: associate investigator Rob Beamish and research assistants Marg MacNeill and Donna Greenhorn. We also wish to thank the executives and the staff of the six national sport organizations in which we did our research for their cooperation and support. Ross Bales, Hugh Glynn, and Sue Neill paved the way for our questionnaire survey at the National Sport and Recreation Centre and at Sport Canada: our special thanks to them. A number of people have reviewed parts of our work: Dallas Cullen, Ann Hall, Sue Neill, Diane Palmason, and Trevor Slack. We are grateful for these contributions as well. The final responsibility for the interpretation of the data, however, remains with the authors. In any study of this nature, there will be some who were involved intimately with high-performance sport at the time of our work who will disagree with some of our interpretations. We hope that these people will appreciate that no one perspective is likely to reflect the whole truth in organizations as complicated and diffuse as those in which we worked, but that they still may find some merit in our point of view.

Portions of this book have been drawn from material published previously under the following titles in the following journals and are included here with permission:

"The Professionalization of Canadian Amateur Sport: Questions of Power and Purpose," *Arena Review* 12(2) (1988): 81–96

"Gender and Power: Explanations of Gender Inequalities in Canadian National Sport Organizations," *International Review for the Sociology of Sport* 24(2) (May 1989): 139–50

"Rational Planning vs Regional Interests: The Professionalization of Canadian Amateur Sport," *Canadian Public Policy*

"The Scientization of Physical Education: Discourses of Performance," Quest 42(1) (1990)

"Equity in Canadian High-Performance Sport: High Performance vs Social Policy," *CAHPER Journal* (in press)

The Game Planners

CHAPTER ONE

Setting the Stage

The manner in which sport is viewed and the relationship between sport and government have changed dramatically in Canada since World War II. For most of Canada's history, sport was envisaged as an activity which provided diversion and amusement for the general populace, but one which had little broader significance. Thus, any government involvement in sport beyond control and prohibitive legislation was seen as being inappropriate. This view of sport is nicely captured in a remark by MP Douglas Fisher when he opened discussion in Parliament on "the very touchy field of sport and international sport." Fisher acknowledged that many saw this (sport) as "a frivolous thing on which to spend money" (HC *Debates*, 21 December 1957: 2750).

But these views and attitudes were to change dramatically. At the conclusion of World War II, the Soviet Union, perhaps in anticipation of the Cold War, began to conceive of sport as a means of demonstrating the achievements of its socialist society and of achieving good will in non-aligned and third-world countries. Other Eastern European socialist countries soon followed suit. Initially, this movement was resisted by Western industrialized nations, in part because of strong residual attachments to the Victorian concept of the "gentleman" amateur athlete. Another reason was that although professional sport as entertainment was becoming an accepted part of the business world, the idea that sport could play a political role was still an alien one. However, the political payoff that the Soviet Union reaped from its international sporting triumphs in the 1950s and the 1960s broke down these resistances. Soon, most of the Western industrialized nations and some third-world countries followed the example of the Soviet Union and some of its Eastern Bloc allies, and commenced to support and train a corps of elite international athletes.

At the same time, this internationalization of sport was accentuated by the advent of television. Sport, it turned out, had a particular affinity for this new medium; it provided live and compelling drama for the home viewer, with suspense and uncertainty about the outcome. Close-ups, instant replays, and simultaneous images of different aspects of the action added to the inherent attraction of the contest. Soon, sporting events were being transmitted into the living rooms of millions of people who, hitherto, had had little knowledge of, or interest in, the type of competitive sports that were so suited to television. This exacerbated and inflamed the international rivalry that was developing in sport between the Soviet Union and the United States and, indeed, among many nations around the world. Canada was no exception. As a result of the astounding victories that the Soviet Union achieved in international hockey championships in the 1950s, Canadian supremacy in this arena was usurped. Growing consternation and concern was expressed, both in the news media and in the House of Commons. For these and other reasons (cf. Macintosh et al. 1987b, chaps. 2 and 4, for a fuller account of these developments), the Canadian government became involved in the promotion of sport.

This formal federal government involvement in the promotion of sport had its origin in 1961 with the passage of the Fitness and Amateur Sport Act. In the early years of the act, however, the government's role was passive and indirect, consisting mainly of federal-provincial cost-sharing agreements to promote mass fitness and sport programs, and of grants to the national sport organizations (NSOs). But as sport assumed an increasingly important role in Canadian popular culture, the government's attitude changed. In a federal election campaign speech in 1968, Prime Minister Pierre Trudeau argued that sport, like other cultural forms which demonstrated Canadian accomplishments, could serve as a powerful source of national unity. Trudeau's election promise to establish a Task Force on Sport was fulfilled in 1968; on the basis of many of the Task Force recommendations, the federal government embarked in the 1970s on a course of direct promotion of what was to become known as high-performance sport.

These events were to have a great impact on the NSOs. They had been criticized in the *Report of the Task Force on Sport for Canadians* (Canada 1969) for their "kitchen table" style of operation. NSOs, according to the Task Force, were characterized by part-time volunteer officers and officials, national executives that were drawn from only one or two regions of the country, and by a high degree of inefficiency. In order to address these deficiencies, the government established the National Sport and Recreation Centre (NSRC) in Ottawa. At the same time, two new divisions, Recreation Canada and Sport Canada, were established within the Fitness and Amateur Sport Branch. The NSRC provided office and support services and Sport Canada provided funds to hire full-time executive, technical, and program directors and national coaches for the NSOs, something which they hitherto had been unable to afford. It is not surprising, therefore, that the administrative, technical, and clerical staff in the NSRC in Ottawa grew from 65 in 1970 to 532 in 1984, and in the same time period, the Fitness and Amateur Sport Branch staff quadrupled in size from 30 to 121 (Macintosh et al. 1987b: 157).

As a result of these developments, the NSOs, which previously had enjoyed a great deal of autonomy in their operations and policy making, changed dramatically. They increased their technical and administrative capacities greatly and they enjoyed enlarged financial resources provided by government. At the same time, however, these organizations experienced a diminution of their traditional autonomy and were unable to develop a cohesive strategy to balance the growing federal government presence in sport. In addition, the two new levels of full-time staff, one in Sport Canada and the second in the NSRC, added a new complexity to the operation of NSOs. We expand on these changes and developments in chapter 3.

These visible changes to the organization and control of high-performance sport in Canada led to some research concerning the relationship of the Canadian federal government and high-performance sport. Studies by Beamish (1978; 1985) and Hollands and Gruneau (1979) focused upon the composition of the voluntary national executive members of the major sport organizations housed in the NSRC in Ottawa. Work by West (1973) and Westland (1979) on the history of federal government involvement in sport and recreation set the stage for subsequent research which linked that history to a variety of broader social, cultural, and political themes (Broom and Baka 1978; Hallett 1981; Macintosh et al. 1987b). These latter studies have mapped out the general framework in which the federal government interacts with NSOs in the making of policy for high-performance sport in Canada. This work suggests that there are five levels to the formal structure that supports high-performance sport at the national level in Canada, as follows:

1   the federal government, and in particular, the cabinet and the minister of state for fitness and amateur sport;

2 the federal sport bureaucracy, and in particular, the assistant deputy minister responsible for sport, the director-general of Sport Canada, and the sport consultants who work with the NSOs;

3 the sport bureaucracy at the NSRC in Ottawa, and in particular, the executive, technical, and program directors of NSOs housed in the Centre;

4 the NSOs and umbrella associations such as the Canadian Olympic Association and the Sports Federation of Canada, and in particular, the voluntary executive members of these groups;

5 key actors outside the formal structure above who have influenced policy making in NSOs. These include influential provincial voluntary executive members and technical and executive directors, current and former sport participants, and other influential national figures associated with the sport.

On the basis of this previous work, it is now possible to focus on more specific settings and examine the policy-making process more concretely. The senior staff officers in NSOs play a very influential role in determining sport policy. First, they hold a central position in any communications between Sport Canada and their respective national executives. Second, they bring to their jobs specialized managerial and technical competencies. As a result, they are in a position to exercise a powerful degree of influence in any struggles over organization policy and direction. These advantages are further augmented because these staff officers hold full-time positions with clerical and research support, whereas voluntary national executive members must respond with less time and support.

It was in this environment and setting that we undertook a study of policy making in six selected NSOs in Ottawa. We had originally planned to focus on the policy-making process and on the central role of the full-time staff officers in these organizations. Not surprisingly, we found that the manner in which these policies were established, the backgrounds and attitudes of those who formulated the policies, and the interactions of these organizations with outside bodies, and in particular, with the federal government, all had a great effect on the practice of sport in Canada. However, the further we progressed with our interviews with key actors in these organizations, the more we were struck by the way in which the outcomes of this policy-making process intersected with larger social and political issues of concern not only to those involved in sport but to all Canadians.

In the chapters that follow, we discuss sport policy making in the six selected NSOs in relation to these larger issues and questions. Those parts of our interviews that focused on the conflicting demands of mass versus elite sport programs almost invariably led to the quadrennial planning process which the federal government imposed on NSOs. Here, the full-time staff members' belief in the rational planning model instituted by Sport Canada and in their own central role in this "quadrennial planning" process contrasted with the scepticism with which many volunteer NSO executive members viewed the quadrennial planning exercise and the concern that these volunteers felt over the erosion of their own roles. This tension surrounding the appropriate roles of "professionals" vis-à-vis "volunteers" brought out the greatest divergence of opinion between staff members and the volunteer executive members among all the issues we raised in our interviews. We elaborate on the "professionalization" theme in chapter 4.

An unexpected conflict, between regional interests and the preservation of regional representation in policy-making structures on the one hand and "the national interest" and the development of nationally oriented decision-making bodies on the other, ran through most of the deliberations and debates in the NSOs. This was particularly evident in the development of quadrennial planning, where, in the interest of efficiency and better performance outcomes, the centrally located staff members and Sport Canada consultants argued for more centralization of coaching and technical resources, and for representation on national executive committees that would be based on technical and professional expertise rather than on provincial and regional considerations. That this thrust was resisted by those whose allegiance was regional and whose biases were for more provincial autonomy and a diversification of coaching and training resources is not surprising. It is another manifestation of the central political debate in Canada since the 1960s, that of federal- provincial relationships and the relative sharing of power and resources between these two levels of government. This struggle, and its implications for NSOs and for the type of sport that will be produced in Canada in the future, are examined and discussed in chapter 5.

The matter of female participation in the mainstream of decision making in both the private and public sectors has become a central and controversial issue in Canadian society. The data we gathered bring specific quantitative and qualitative information to bear on the issue of advancement of females to higher-level technical, administrative, and policy-making positions in sport. We relate these findings to current theories about gender relations and to models for change in the work-place in chapter 6.

The data we gathered also intersect with two other areas of inequity in Canadian society. First, francophones were substantially underrepresented in the ranks of staff members at the NSRC in Ottawa. Other studies suggest that this underrepresentation also extends to volunteer executive members of NSOs and to the ranks of Canada's high-performance athletes. Our data about the socio-economic class background of the sport administrators in Ottawa also led to questions about the persistent underrepresentation of persons from working-class backgrounds in the ranks of Canada's high-performance athletes. This underrepresentation continues in spite of statements in federal government sport policy documents in past years that equality of opportunity in sport for all Canadians is one of its avowed goals. Our interview data suggested that whenever there was a conflict between social policy or equity-oriented objectives and the narrower "performance" objectives of high-performance sport, it was accomplishing the latter that most staff and volunteer executive members assumed to be their primary task. Our conversations with these people suggested that they simply did not see sport policy as an aspect of social policy. Neither was sport recognized as a public institution in which officials have the same responsibilities to promote equity as they would have in other public institutions. We present these data and discuss these issues in chapter 7. Then, in chapter 8, we relate these equity issues to theories of the welfare state and examine how much freedom of action is available to these sport administrators, individually and collectively, within the structures of Canadian public policy.

In chapter 9, we return to the issue of professionalization and postulate that the evolution of sport management "professionals" as central agents in the national sport bureaucracy is partly an outcome of the reconstruction of the physical education profession, in which the language and, ultimately, the objectives of "sport science" and "sport management" come to be taken for granted. We consider these sport professionals to be products of specific changes in the physical education profession, and of broader changes which have constructed new roles for "experts" in many Canadian institutions once run by volunteers, and, indeed, in many spheres of Canadian life. We also consider whether a "deconstruction" of these new discourses could generate discussion on a different set of issues among those (staff members and volunteers) who might have misgivings about the erosion of democracy that has become a part of the new world of high-performance sport.

In the final chapter, we summarize and integrate the issues raised in previous chapters and advance some modest proposals which we believe would help make sport a more equitable and fair terrain for all Canadians. In the epilogue to the last chapter, we relate these issues and our analysis of them to the matters raised in the Dubin inquiry on the use of performance-enhancing drugs in Canadian high-performance sport. First, however, we review the theories that shaped our own understandings of what is at stake in the developments outlined above. Then, in chapter 3, we turn to a history of the relationship between NSOs and the federal government.

CHAPTER TWO

Theoretical Frameworks

The theoretical frameworks which inform our work are drawn from four related areas of concern within sociology and political studies. At the broadest level, we draw our general conception of society and of social reproduction and change from the recent work of Giddens (1979; 1984), Thompson (1984; 1987), Offe (1984; 1985), and Habermas (1971; 1972). Thus, we view the rationalization of successive social institutions (including sport) as the product of knowledgeable agents (collective as well as individual) who compete and negotiate with one another in the context of existing social structures. We use "structures" here to refer to structures of language and public discourse as well as to structures of relationships between men and women. The results of these competitions and negotiations reflect relative access to power and are predisposed towards the continued production and reproduction of patterned social relations (e.g., class and gender relations). These latter structures or enduring patterns enable and constrain individuals in characteristic ways according to their own particular social location (cf. the work of Giddens and Thompson). It is from this sort of framework that we wish to examine the formation of a new kind of Canadian sport management "professional" and the type of impact it is having on Canadian sport.

It is important to situate our own work here within a growing corpus of critical sport sociology and sport history. Ingham (1975) was the first to attempt to apply the analyses which major sociologists like Weber and Marcuse had developed of rationalization, as a broad socio-historical process, to the study of sport. "Rationalization," as used by Weber, refers to a historical process in which successive human institutions are subjected to "scientific" analysis, and are reshaped so as to increase efficiency and productivity. Technical rationalization, in this context, refers to the refinement of technique itself and to the more efficient use of technical resources. Bureaucratic rationalization refers to the quest to make *organizations* more productive, and to the reorganization of administration so that productivity can be measured and enhanced there too. We will see both of these processes in sport.

Ingham suggested specifically that Weber's analysis of the growth of bureaucracy in many kinds of work organization was clearly applicable to sport. Moreover, it drew attention to the appeal that rationalization, *as a methodological principle*, had for those whose interest was in increasing productivity in a whole variety of human activities. Beyond this, though, he also drew on Marcuse's discussion of the ascendancy of the "performance principle" in industrial capitalist societies – the idea that "results orientation" is appropriate to every human activity, and that productivity gains justify the reorganization of any and all activities – to suggest that rationalization gradually became an end in itself, a "good thing," rather than simply a means to an end. Together, Ingham proposed, these insights point to a historical process in which both technical and bureaucratic rationalization came to be seen as desirable in a succession of social institutions which, until this period in history, had developed along traditional lines (cf. also Habermas 1971). The result was that these institutions, which Ingham demonstrates included sport, became more performance oriented, and that the demands of the rationalized pursuit of higher performance levels helped to legitimate new structures of control.

Similar themes are also found in the work of Guttmann (1978), and Gruneau (1983; 1988). The former traces the transformation of sports from a diverse collection of physical contests associated with community celebrations into a group of codified and formally organized institutions that are highly performance oriented and in which performance standards have risen dramatically as a result of technical and bureaucratic rationalization. What Guttmann terms the "modernization" of sport has its dark sides, such as violence and the use of performance-enhancing drugs. Guttmann considers these able to be policed, however, and he portrays modernization as on balance beneficial and, in any event, historically inevitable.

Gruneau takes the position that the uncritical representation of pushing back the frontiers of sporting performance as "progress" obscures issues of freedom and domination which were highlighted more effectively in the Ingham/Marcuse/Habermas analyses. He suggests that the transmutation of playful physical contests into performance oriented, commercial sport was both enabling and constraining. At the level of the activity itself, more demanding norms of skill and fitness, along with the spread of knowledge as to how to achieve these, made possible experiences of mastery that were arguably more intense and more widely diffused in the population. However, the practice of sport became necessarily disciplined and standardized, in ways that impinged upon the freedom and spontaneity nominally associated with play. At another level, moreover, the material and ideological benefits that success in sport at the highest levels promises (to corporations and governments, as well as individual performers) offers unprecedented opportunities to those with the resources to compete in this league. Again, however, the corollaries are tendencies towards oligopoly and towards organizational constraint and discipline, each of which was also highlighted in Ingham's analyses of the world of North American professional sport.

Gruneau was concerned, then, that the rationalization of sport not be celebrated uncritically. He argued, moreover, that occurring as it did in Canada within historically specific class structures, the modernization of sport was part of a larger modernization of Canadian social structures which remained class structures at the same time that their legitimating rhetoric became increasingly meritocratic. He demonstrated that up to and into the 1970s, the dominant groups in Canadian society remained firmly in control of Canadian sport. If experiences in sport and especially in leadership positions in sport could be considered empowering experiences, these remained more readily available to middle- and upper-class anglophone males. The analysis of the development of modern sport, in other words, could not be bracketed off from the analysis of socio-historical process and from the central sociological questions of power and structure (cf. Hargreaves 1986, for an analysis of sport in Britain which raises similar themes, as well as Critcher 1986, for a commentary on both Gruneau and Hargreaves).

Within this general analysis of power and structure, our second focus is on the role of the state in Canadian high-performance sport; here, we draw upon the rapidly expanding literature on the state in industrial capitalist societies. Two themes in this literature are at the heart of our work. First, the reach of state activity has extended far beyond the minimal functions indicated in classical models of government. The growth of state spending and of state management of the economy need not be detailed here. What is pertinent is that state interventions in sport and recreation can be analysed as particular instances of broader negotiations over the levels and objectives of public spending and over the structures within which public policy decisions are made. In the latter case, the issue is the extent to which the rationalization of planning structures and the greater involvement of experts results in the insulation of successive areas of decision making from the pressures of democratic, interest group politics. Conversely, the question can be posed as the extent to which: "specialists and their knowledge remain accountable to the general cultural knowledge and to the interests of the group whom they are advising" (Misgeld 1985: 107–8).

There is much to be learned about the question of the accountability of "experts" from the descriptions and analyses of the structures and real practices of policy formation in other state agencies in Canada that operate within contexts similar to that of sport (cf. Banting 1987; Milne 1986). We start from the premise that to talk of "the state" now extends well beyond directly "political" activities, and that it is often difficult to demarcate the political from the administrative. The state now includes a range of administrative institutions whose personnel are themselves skilled and knowledgeable agents, who are often highly committed to their own collective projects, whether these are regional development or high-performance sport. The professional staff in the National Sport and Recreation Centre in Ottawa who are the focus of this study are simply particular instances of this phenomenon. At the same time, however, all agents of the state, whether politicians or public servants, are subject to political and economic constraints that influence them in powerful and often contradictory ways, and place limits both on what they can accomplish and on what they believe they can attempt (cf. Offe 1984; Thompson 1984). Again, there is a small but growing literature on sport and the state which begins with Cantelon and Gruneau (1982), in which several contributors attempted to make sense of the growing involvement of Western states in high-performance sport, with reference to then current debates in political economy and state theory. Harvey (1988) makes a significant contribution towards updating these debates in relation to assaults on the welfare state in the 1980s.

Thirdly, and at a more concrete level of analysis, our work draws on the now extensive literature on professionalization and considers the professionalization of high-performance sport in Canada as simply another instance of the emergence of many new professions and "semi-professions," each connected with the establishment of new forms of specialist knowledge and new kinds of credentials. In referring to the professionalization of Canadian sport, we do not mean, of course, the athletes themselves, but rather the evolution within provincial and national government departments and sport organizations of paid administrative and technical specialists. The function of these new "professionals" is to pursue the development of their sport and their organization in more systematic and expert ways than was the case when these matters were in the hands of volunteer executive members of sport organizations. At the same time, we also refer to the emergence of new kinds of technical and administrative careers that are now available in high-performance sport to those who can offer appropriate combinations of specialist experience and credentials.

The early literature on the professions (cf. Hughes 1958; Parsons 1968) tended to stress the growing significance of knowledge in the modern economy, in public administration, and in new forms of "caring work." Some authors have examined the activities of specific professional groups and have considered the possibility that rhetoric which articulated "professionalism" with public service had a self-serving function as well (cf. Bledstein 1976; Geison 1983). However, sociological analysis of professionalization was preoccupied for a long time with establishing the definitive attributes of professions and with using these to assess the claims of different occupational groups to professional status (cf. Hughes 1958; cf. also Veysey 1975, for a trenchant critique of this "attributional" approach).

Some people involved in sport administration and management programs draw upon this attributional approach to object to the use of the term "professional" to describe the people who staff the NSOs in Ottawa, on the grounds that they do not possess common educational qualifications or have any certification standards or code of professional ethics. However, we argue both that there are good grounds for treating the persons working in the national sport structure as at least "aspirant professionals" and that to do so offers important insights into the power struggles and the issues of principle that our interviews uncovered. Here, it is sufficient to observe that although the best of this attributional literature did raise questions about the wider implications of the rise of technical and bureaucratic rationality (cf. Wilensky 1964), for the most part the growth of new professions and of new forms of specialized knowledge were portrayed as both inevitable and beneficial. The serious application of knowledge in successive areas of human endeavours seemed to require an increasingly specialized division of intellectual labour, and the new levels of achievement that this promised were broadly seen as "progress."

This largely benign view of professionalization came under fire from scholars whose focus of interest was the increasingly powerful structural location of professions and professionals in key areas of public life (cf. Freidson 1970; Johnson 1972). Marxist and other versions of conflict theory were also utilized to ground a more critical analysis of professionalization as "an attempt to translate one order of scarce resources – special knowledge and skills – into another, social and economic rewards" (Larson 1977, xvii). This view of professionalization as a series of collective and self-interested "projects" (Larson's term) was also linked, in most analyses based in conflict theory, to historical struggles between emerging educated elites and older elites, whose power base was elsewhere (e.g., in tradition, capital, party loyalty, ideological purity). Such struggles have concerned the social organization and uses of knowledge, and the social position of intellectuals and technical specialists in the emerging "knowledge-based" society (cf. Bledstein 1976; Collins 1978; Larson 1977). It is in the sense of this specialized knowledge and privileged position that we henceforth use the term "professional" to refer to those people who hold administrative and technical positions in NSOs and who are sport consultants with Sport Canada.

There is disagreement between those who argue that the new powers deriving from the mastery of specialist forms of knowledge and from the privileged status that knowledge now generally enjoys have together produced a "new class" with its own collective interests to advance (Gouldner 1979; Konrad and Szelenyi 1979), and those who do not see the control accruing to experts within formally structured democratic institutions as being an important political issue (Bell 1976). However, there is broad agreement about the significance of knowledge in industrial capitalist societies. In our work, we draw from both sides of this debate to formulate a series of questions concerning the nature of the power of professional staff within Canada's national sport structure. These lead to hypotheses about the impact of such professionals on Canadian sport policy and about the nature of their interactions with other groups who have legitimate interests in the shaping of that policy.

Our fourth level of analysis, which makes connections among all the previous three, is based in a critical theory of ideology. This theory sees ideologies as products of human practice, but, at the same time, as special products that in turn contour the ideas and the conceptual structures that we have readily available to us. They thereby exert a powerful "structuring" effect on how we learn to conceive of social institutions and of our own possible relations to them. In relation to the first body of theory mentioned above (the mutually constitutive relationships between structures and agents), our point here is that studying the language in which we learn to talk about social relations (i.e., patterned relationships between men and women, for example, or between experts and lay persons) can offer a fresh perspective on the apparent "naturalness" of these relationships themselves. It invites us to consider the extent to which received ideas about social relations are themselves products of those relations. At the same time, studying the specialist language that experts use to discuss what they do (in a sport, for example, or indeed, in management) can reveal the impact of specialist discourses on popular understandings, and thus, how professionals' formulations of institutional purposes come to be widely taken for granted. In both cases, as Thompson (1987) suggests, to study ideologies with such questions in mind is to inquire into the uses of ideas in the reproduction and transformation of social institutions.

In particular relation to state theory, our interest is in the use of ideology by politicians and by many different kinds of administrative and policy agencies, including the Fitness and Amateur Sport Branch, to establish what have become widely held (although seldom unchallenged) understandings of their own roles in particular aspects of Canadian life. More generally, we are also interested in the establishment (as well as the contesting) of "orthodox" views concerning the role of government in public life, and conversely, the role of citizens in the making of public policy at a time when government has become increasingly the preserve of experts and professional public servants.

This, in turn, leads us back to professionalization, where our interest is in the place of ideology in the project of establishing a new profession (in this case, the sport management careers described above), and the impact of professional ideologies in shaping popular understandings of a host of public issues, including health care and environmental issues as well as sport issues (Forester 1985). We are also interested in the ideological construction of professionals themselves, for we believe that Geison is correct in proposing that conflict-based analyses of professionalization have sometimes overstated the presence of self-interest in claims for the significance of new forms of expertise. Our reading of professionalization in Canadian sport, indeed, reinforced Geison's contention (1983): "professionals have usually constructed their ideologies unself-consciously and sincerely, that whatever deception may be embodied in professional ideology and rhetoric is partly a matter of self-deception as well" (ibid., 7). This only underlines, however, the importance of a careful examination of what the professional staff in the NSOs believe about themselves and an analysis of how orthodox understandings of their roles in Canadian sport are constructed and made popular (see chaps. 4 and 9).

In the next chapter, we turn to a brief history of the relationship between the federal government and the NSOs. The reader is referred to appendix A for a brief exposition of the methodological approach to our study.

CHAPTER THREE

The Federal Government and National Sport Organizations

HISTORICAL PERSPECTIVE

The greatly increased significance of sport in Canadian society which came about after World War II and which caused the federal government to become formally involved in the promotion of sport was to change irrevocably the nature of national sport organizations (NSOs) (cf. Macintosh 1988). Prior to this time, these organizations had enjoyed a great deal of autonomy, but their activities had been of interest to only a small minority of people in Canada; thus, they operated with little attention or concern on the part of government or the public. After the passage of the Fitness and Amateur Sport Act (Bill C-131) in 1961, the federal government was content to adopt a "hands off" attitude towards the NSOs and allowed the National Fitness and Amateur Sport Advisory Council, a body established by Bill C-131 to advise the government on sport and physical fitness, to deal with these organizations. This the council did, largely by making grants of money to help finance national championships and meetings of national executives and to make improvements in coaching.

But these measures did little to improve the performances of Canada's international athletes. The clamours about Canada's poor showings that had helped bring about Bill C-131 continued unabated in the 1960s. Thus, when Pierre Trudeau's Task Force on Sport was established in 1968, the time was ripe for direct government involvement in the promotion of high-performance sport. John Munro, then minister of health and welfare, who had responsibilities for fitness and amateur sport, was a strong advocate of government involvement in high-performance sport. He took it upon himself, with the urging and support of Lou Lefaive, then director of fitness and amateur sport, to move forward with a number of recommendations from the report of the task force even before this report had been tabled in the House of Commons.

Two of these measures, the establishment of the National Sport and Recreation Centre (NSRC) in Ottawa, and the inauguration of the Coaching Association of Canada, were to have a profound effect on the NSOs. The NSRC provided a central location for all national sport associations who wished to locate there, and as well, provided free office accommodation and secretarial and other support services to these organizations. At the same time, Sport Canada provided the funds for NSOs to hire full-time staff members to support their operations. As was pointed out in chapter 1, the "kitchen table" style of management of the NSOs had been a focal point of criticism in the task force report. Some thirty-three NSOs were in residence when the NSRC moved into its permanent location in May 1971. By 1978–79, there were fifty-seven sport organizations in-house and the operating budget for the national centre was some $3 million (Macintosh et al. 1987b: 89).

The NSOs flourished in this new environment, growing rapidly in size and complexity (see the figures given in chapter 1) and in their capacity to provide technical and administrative support to athletes and coaches in their respective sports. In cooperation with provincial governments and the respective provincial sport associations, the NSOs and the Coaching Association of Canada went to work to put in place a national coaching certification program, an accomplishment that was the envy of the "amateur" sport community in many other Western nations who were striving to improve their own quality of coaching. The close proximity of the NSOs under one roof allowed them to support and to learn from one another. But this close proximity to the major source of their funds, the federal government, was to contribute to a gradual, but steady, loss of autonomy that the NSOs experienced in the 1970s and the 1980s.

A number of other developments during these years were also to contribute to the decline in autonomy that accompanied these years of growth. First, there was a gradual change in status of international athletes from that of "amateur" to that of paid employee of the state, and, in some cases, to that of private entrepreneur. This evolution started in the Soviet-bloc countries in the 1950s and was followed, although to varying degrees and in different manners, by many of the Western industrialized nations in the 1960s and 1970s. This development was to have a profound impact on the practice of sport in Canada and in the status of the NSOs. The matter of financial support for Canada's athletes had been in the air ever since the passage of the Fitness and Amateur Sport Act in

1961. Indeed, John Munro's *Proposed Sports Policy for Canadians* (1970) had resulted in the implementation of a grants-in-aid program, which provided financial support for athletes while they were students. This program, however, did not recognize the problems that non-university athletes were having in trying to combine sport training with holding a regular job.

One of the major recommendations that came out of the National Conference on Olympic '76 Development, held in Ottawa in 1971, was a resolution calling for financial aid for Canada's elite coaches and athletes. As a result, Sport Canada initiated an "Intensive Care" program in 1972 to provide monies for potential medal-winners in the 1972 Olympic Games. This plan was seen by most sport officials as being "too little, too late" to have any real impact on athlete performance in the 1972 Olympics. But the fact that the 1976 Summer Olympics were to be staged in Montreal was to be the motivation for the next escalation of aid to athletes in Canada. In 1972, the Canadian Olympic Association (COA) announced its intention to provide support to Canada's high-performance athletes through a plan which was to be called "Game Plan '76." This plan was unique in the annals of Canadian sport in that it had the support not only of the COA and the federal government but of all the provincial governments and most of the important multi-sport organizations as well.

In 1974, the International Olympic Committee (IOC) changed its eligibility regulations to allow for lost-time income to compensate athletes for monies lost while they were away from their jobs training. The following spring, a group of athletes (including Abby Hoffman, the current director-general of Sport Canada, and Bruce Kidd, prominent sport historian and activist) petitioned the COA for payments consistent with this new IOC regulation. The nature of this new provision was such that the federal government felt it could not risk reimbursing athletes directly for lost-time income, so the COA took on this and some other direct-aid program responsibilities while the federal government assumed financial responsibility for the original Game Plan operations. Some idea of the magnitude of the assistance to athletes can be seen in the following figures. In the nine-month period leading up to the 1976 Montreal Games, the COA provided some $584,000 to support 348 athletes (Beamish and Borowy 1987: 14). In 1975–76, the federal government expended some $3.7 million on Game Plan (Macintosh et al. 1987b: 88).

The promise of financial support for Game Plan from the provinces did not materialize; only Ontario and Quebec made payments in the early years. In December 1975, the provinces agreed among themselves to terminate their involvement in Game Plan. Following the 1976 Olympics, the COA confined its role to the assistance of club athletes who were not supported by scholarships, and the federal government assumed full responsibility for the continuation of Game Plan as well as maintaining its grants-in-aid program to student athletes.

In 1980, after conducting a review of its two athlete support programs, Sport Canada consolidated them under the auspices of its new Athlete Assistance Program (AAP). At this time, the process by which aid was tied to performance, something that had been evolving during the second half of the 1970s, was intensified. Sport Canada financial support became contingent on a formal rating system, based on the athlete's or the team's world rankings in international competition. This aid was confined largely to athletes in Olympic sports. In addition, Sport Canada took over from the NSOs the responsibility for making these payments to the athletes and commenced to mail out the cheques and to communicate directly with the athletes themselves. This occurred in spite of objections from many NSOs, who felt that this was clearly their own responsibility. For a full exposition of the history of financial aid to athletes in Canada, the reader is referred to Beamish and Borowy (1987).

By 1985–86, the federal government's budget for the AAP amounted to some $4.5 million. Thus, the federal government found itself in the position of controlling directly the support funds and the criteria under which funds were paid to Canada's high-performance athletes; the NSOs, who were ostensibly responsible for the development of their sport, were left in a subservient role.

Another factor which contributed to the decline in autonomy of the NSOs was the extent to which most of them became largely dependent on the federal government for their financial support. Some NSOs, either because of the financial stature of their membership or their ability, in a climate of increased interest in their sport, to attract private-sector sponsors, were able to find at least some significant part of their budgets from sources other than the public coffers. But most NSOs became largely dependent on the federal government for their funds. This left them very vulnerable to the threats of fund withdrawal that became the trade mark of the federal government's dealings with NSOs in the 1980s whenever there was a disagreement over sport policy. The reader is referred to chapter 8 in Macintosh et al. (1987b) for the particulars of this development.

Some idea of the extent of this financial dependence on the federal government may be seen in the following figures compiled by the Sport Marketing Council (1986: 1). Of the sixty-six NSOs surveyed in this study, fifteen relied on the federal government for more than 85 per cent of their total revenues and thirty-five for between 50 and 85 per cent. Only fifteen of these NSOs were able to find more than 50 per cent of their total revenues from non-governmental sources. Obviously, those sport organizations with high public profiles were more able to raise monies from private sponsors. But even in such NSOs, dependency remained surprisingly high because expanding programming required increasing levels of support from both public and private sectors. In swimming, for instance, a sport with a high profile that was able to attract private sponsors, Swimming Canada Natation, as this NSO is now called, still depended on the federal government for about half of its funds in 1985–86. For the Canadian Track and Field Association, this figure in 1984–85 was 68 per cent (Macintosh et al. 1987a: 167,309).

Another factor that impinged on the autonomy of the NSOs was the ambivalent position of the full-time administrative and technical staff of these associations. Because their salaries were paid largely from grants by Sport Canada earmarked specifically for this purpose, the professional staff found themselves with divided loyalties between the agency that paid their salaries and the organization that they had been hired to represent. Thus, in many of the debates between the federal government and the NSOs about the direction of sport policy in Canada, the interests of the sport organizations themselves were not always actively represented by their professional staff (cf. Macintosh 1988).

This imbalance of power in the relationship between the federal government and the NSOs has been long recognized by many as one of the weaknesses of Canada's high-performance sport system. Thus, it is not surprising that there have been a number of attempts since the federal government's intrusion in Canada's sport system in 1970 to bring together under one umbrella all of the NSOs and the important multi-sport organizations, such as the COA and the Canadian Interuniversity Athletic Union, so that one strong and independent organization could speak for sport and stand up to the federal government. For a detailed account of these attempts, the reader is referred to an analysis of the recent relationships between the federal government and the NSOs by Macintosh (1988).

It suffices to say that none of these unification efforts was successful. One reason certainly was that the most concerted and lengthy of these efforts was spearheaded by the COA, and many of the NSOs perceived this to be an attempt by a powerful and relatively independent multi-sport organization to gain control of the proposed umbrella organization. Another reason was that many of the most powerful of the NSOs were not enthusiastic about such an umbrella group because they believed they might better "get their way" with the federal government by using their own lobbying abilities. As well, the larger of the NSOs with relatively high profiles were reluctant to give up any autonomy to an organization that would give equal rights and voting powers to the relatively large number of small, little-known NSOs that were often the champions of these unification efforts. Another more controversial view of the failure of the sport community to attain its goal of a strong, unified body is that these efforts received at best only lukewarm support from the federal government. A continued weak and divided sport community meant that the federal government could continue to have its way in its relationships with the NSOs.

Perhaps the most instructive example of the consequences of this divisiveness in the sport community was the cross-country hearings that Iona Campagnolo, the first minister of state for fitness and amateur sport, scheduled in late 1977 and early 1978 to vet her green paper, *Toward a National Policy on Amateur Sport: A Working Paper* (Campagnolo 1977). This was the first and only opportunity that NSOs and other interested parties were to have to react formally and publicly to a federal government policy initiative on sport. But instead of presenting some kind of a common front, each NSO and multi-sport organization went about its own way, presenting separate and, in many instances, contrary views about the direction sport should take in Canada in the 1980s. The result was that Campagnolo was able to take what she wished from these briefs in preparing the resulting white paper, *Partners in Pursuit of Excellence: A National Policy on Amateur Sport* (Campagnolo 1979). The final product disappointed most and pleased very few. Some would argue that the outcome would have been much the same even if the sport community had been more unified. But a more optimistic view is that Campagnolo would have had to pay much more attention to any recommendations coming out of a united front.

A more recent development, quadrennial planning, has also served to strengthen the grip that the federal government holds on the NSOs. This planning process, which required all NSOs that represent Olympic sports to develop a detailed four-year plan leading up to the 1988 Olympics, probably had its origins in the rational planning concept that Pierre Trudeau brought with him to the federal government when he came to the office of prime minister in 1968. But this rational planning did not surface in sport until the early 1980s with the federal government announcement that it would set aside some $25 million for use by the ten Winter Olympic sport organizations in order to ensure a "best ever" performance by Canadian athletes in the Calgary Winter Olympics. These funds were awarded on top of the regular Sport Canada annual appropriations to the NSOs and in addition to the some $200 million that the federal government had committed to the capital and operating costs of staging the Winter Olympics in Calgary. This "Best Ever '88" program represented the first official commitment of government funds to NSOs for a period longer than one year. This commitment carried along with it a requirement on the part of each of the ten NSOs involved to develop a four-year plan which would improve the organization's technical and administrative capacities to produce high-performance athletes.

In August of 1984, the federal government made political capital from the successes of Canadian athletes at the Los Angeles Summer Olympics by announcing that it would extend the "Best Ever" Winter Program to the 1988 Summer Games in Seoul.

It set aside a sum of $38 million to be used by summer Olympic sport organizations to bolster their capacities to produce medal-winners at the 1988 Summer Olympics. Thus, the planning process which had been initiated with the winter Olympic sports was extended to those NSOs that would be involved with the 1988 Summer Olympics. In 1981–82, Sport Canada had initiated a review of the status of the technical programs and the financial requirements of ten "successful" Olympic sport organizations. This High-Performance Sport Task Force, not surprisingly, concluded that no model or system for the development of high-performance athletes existed in most NSOs.

These events set the stage for the introduction of the quadrennial planning process whereby Sport Canada "invited" Olympic sport NSOs to participate in a planning process leading up to the 1988 Summer Olympics. As a result of the review of the "Best Ever" winter sport planning exercises and the recommendations of the High-Performance Sport Task Force, Sport Canada put into place an elaborate procedure within which this planning process was to take place. Each of the six high-profile Olympic sport NSOs in which we worked in our case studies was intimately involved in this process. It was this issue, quadrennial planning, and the associated struggle between mass sport programs and high-performance sport that provided us with some of the best information about how policy was made in NSOs and gave us valuable insights into the struggles which were occurring in these organizations.

These struggles are discussed in some detail in the chapters that follow. Here, we identify and highlight their major features. First, quadrennial planning brought to the fore the matter of the democratic process within the respective organizations. There were many participants, especially among the volunteer membership, who were sceptical about the extent to which the government was really interested in their input. Quadrennial planning was seen by such people as being imposed by Sport Canada, and with preconceived ideas about the outcomes, so that the organization was simply going through the process of dancing to the federal government's tune.

The quadrennial planning process also brought to a head the issue of the proper role of the full-time professional staff in these organizations. The battle over the appropriate role for these staff members in the management of NSOs and in the taking of policy decisions had been one which had been fought out in almost all of the sport organizations during the late 1970s and the early 1980s, with different results in different NSOs. But, as we pointed out in chapter 2, the pressure brought to bear by Sport Canada for a more rationalized approach to the operation of NSOs appeared, to many volunteer executive members in this planning process, to favour a more dominant and powerful role for the full-time professional staff. This exacerbated the struggle between the paid staff and those in volunteer positions about the respective roles of each in the affairs of the NSOs. This struggle leads to our discussion of the "professionalization" of the national sport bureaucracy in the next chapter.

Another related issue that surfaced in these debates over quadrennial planning and which was also introduced in chapter 2 was that of the appropriate sharing of power between the respective regional sport organizations and their parent central body. Once again, this issue pitted the professional staff and Sport Canada, each advocating a more centralized organizational and policy-making structure, against many of the volunteer executive members, who represented various regions of the organizations, and whose views on this matter, rather naturally, differed from those of their full-time staff and the Sport Canada consultants. This issue is addressed in chapter 5.

This quadrennial planning process also brought into focus the matter of what the legitimate goals of the high-performance mandate within NSOs should be. The single focus of this mandate and the single criterion of success, from the federal government's view, was performance at the 1988 Olympic Games. For many people involved from the NSOs' side, this single focus was inappropriate. In the first instance, it deemphasized other important international events – in particular, the world championships, which for most of these sport organizations were held in off years between the Olympics. Especially in team sports, concentrating all efforts on Olympic years meant that world and other important international championships were occasions where young talent was seasoned and developed, with the outcome downplayed. In other sports such as swimming and track and field, the world championships were of equal, if not greater, importance than the Olympics.

Finally, the focus on the 1988 Olympics, combined with uncertainty about the future of federal government commitment to funding after those Olympics, raised questions in the NSOs about the wisdom of putting all their eggs into that one basket. Certainly, the thrust in the mid-1980s by the then minister of state for fitness and amateur sport, Otto Jelinek, to privatize sport gave more credibility to such doubts. Jelinek announced in 1985 that NSOs would be required to find at least one-half of their funds from non-governmental sources by the fiscal year 1988–89 (Ministry of State, Fitness and Amateur Sport 1985: 7). The shortcomings of this measure are discussed at greater length in Macintosh et al. (1987b: 183–4). Here, it is sufficient to say that such a measure would lead to substantial inequalities among sport organizations in their capacity to raise funds from the private sector. High-profile sports and athletes would receive the lion's share of private sector funding while those sports and athletes that labour with little publicity and public interest would find themselves under severe financial pressure. Although Jelinek's goal was not reached, it was still one of the federal government's objectives in its 1988 sport policy document (Canada 1988: 65).

In the next chapter, we turn to the professionalization of Canada's high-performance sport system. But first the reader is referred to appendix B for a brief description of the demographic characteristics of the professional staff in Ottawa associated with high-performance sport.

CHAPTER FOUR

Professionalization of High-Performance Sport

I INTRODUCTION

In chapter 1, we documented briefly the changes which occurred in the nature and practice of sport after World War II, both in Canada and in Western industrialized nations and Soviet-bloc countries. One of the major changes discussed was the more aggressive and direct role in the promotion of high-performance sport taken by the federal government. In this chapter, we argue that the professionalization of the Canadian high-performance sport system needs to be understood in the same way that the professionalization of a succession of other areas of social life has been explained, that is, as an outcome of efforts on the part of aspiring groups in society to promote new forms and discourses of knowledge, and to translate their mastery of this knowledge into the power and influence of a profession (cf. Brown 1986; Collins 1978; Connell 1983; Haskell 1984).

Our analysis begins with a review of key themes in the sociological literature on the professions and the political implications of professionalization. Our view is that whether one sees the extension of professionalism into new areas of life as a progressive development, or as the self-interested project of specific social groups, or as both at once, it is necessary to grasp how increments in the influence of professionals are negotiated and otherwise accomplished, and to understand the political (indeed, the "depoliticizing") effects of such developments.

In the central part of the chapter, we consider some of the struggles which have surrounded, and still surround, this changing of the guard in the decision-making echelons of Canadian sport. In particular, we examine quadrennial planning as a process which highlighted for us, just as it was designed to highlight for volunteers, that the pursuit of excellence in international sport requires both technical and bureaucratic rationalization in Canadian sport. In this environment, many kinds of decisions once made by amateurs and part-timers in politically structured bodies have effectively been taken over by professionals. Quadrennial planning, however, throws into relief the role of the state in restructuring the management of Canadian NSOs. In doing so, moreover, it allows us to recognize that the depoliticization of Canadian sport institutions has also meant that a series of other, essentially political questions about the social relations of Canadian sport organizations, and about the role of the state in Canadian sport, are effectively submerged.

In the final section of the chapter, we discuss the tensions that attend the professionalization of new and very specific forms of knowledge within quasi-public institutions. Here, we argue that the sponsorship of such experts by the state creates a complicated set of relationships between the professionals, the state, and the client groups whom these experts and, indeed, the state itself are ostensibly serving. This raises questions about the proper role of experts in the formation of public policy. It also raises a more specific set of questions about priorities in Canadian sport: about who is involved in the setting of priorities when, as we shall observe, technical and bureaucratic rationalization can conflict with equity-related objectives that are accepted and well established in Canadian society.

II PROFESSIONS AND
PROFESSIONALIZATION

... we must discriminate those claims to knowledge and skill that are genuinely valuable from those that are not.   (Freidson 1984: 26)

The question to ask about expert power today is ... whether the possession of scientific and technical knowledge can now directly confer political power upon its possessors.   (Larson 1984: 28)

As noted in chapter 2, the early literature on the professions was much concerned with developing lists of traits or attributes which could be used to define what was meant by a "profession," and to test the claims to professional status of a variety of occupational groups (cf. Hughes 1958; Lynn 1965; Vollmer and Mills 1966). The reader is also referred to Cullen (1983) for a recent version of this early literature, which Thibault et al. (1988) have drawn upon to justify treating the technical and administrative personnel in Canadian sport as professionals. This "attributional" approach had a surface plausibility in an era when certified knowledge was being increasingly demanded for many familiar jobs (as well as new and apparently complex ones), and when new divisions of labour were more visibly supplanting older ones. However, as critics have pointed out, the trait approach offers little in the way of explanation for the real power struggles that have typically surrounded the establishment of new occupations and the eclipse of old ones. It offers no sense, moreover, of relationships between occupational structures and structures of class, gender, and ethnicity. Its findings, therefore, have been of little historical or sociological interest (see critiques by Johnson 1972; Roth 1974; Veysey 1975).

Historically, attempts to be definitive about professions are confounded by important cross-cultural variations – for example, in the very different histories of engineering and medicine in the United States and Britain, and, it might be suggested, in the different status coaches have enjoyed in some European countries in comparison to English-speaking nations. The trait or attribute approach also runs up against the fact of historical changes which are common to many countries, in particular the growth of corporate and government employment of professionals (cf. Johnson 1972). Such developments profoundly change the nature of professional-client relations (cf. also Johnston and Robbins 1977) and complicate any notion of "professional autonomy," which the attributional approach has typically proposed as the central characteristic of a profession.

For sociologists, the problem is that debates over whether or not an occupation "qualifies" as a profession contribute little to an understanding of the social and political forces that have produced either new forms of work or new work relations. Neither are such debates germane to any theory that addresses the sociological and political significance of such changes (e.g., for class relations, for gender relations, or for relationships between political, economic, and cultural institutions). We are satisfied that the organizational changes that have occurred in high-performance sport can be described as professionalization, with Slack and Hinings's proviso (1987a) that different sports are at different stages in this process. However, we need to turn to more fully developed theories of social change to help us address the sociological and political concerns alluded to above. Here, as Haskell (1984) suggests, it is, on the one hand, liberal or functionalist theories, which broadly see "modernization" as an adaptive response to "system needs," and, on the other, conflict theories (including Marxism), which see all history (including the history of occupations) as the outcome of ongoing struggles between different interest groups, that vie for prominence in explicating these social changes. Both functionalist and conflict theories encompass considerable variations in emphasis, but together they structure the parameters of the debate.

Functionalist theorists have stressed the growing significance of knowledge and, beyond this, of task-specific expertise in enhancing the productivity of the economy and public administration alike. They see the conditions necessary for such enhancement as follows: the expansion of advanced (and applied) education; the application of scientific analysis to a succession of social as well as technical problems; and a division of labour which permits high degrees of task specialization. As a result, we now enjoy a productive economy and a "modern" society, a society which offers more opportunities to more people than did its predecessors (cf. Bell 1976; Parsons 1954). It is acknowledged that technological and bureaucratic rationalization have meant the eclipse of many traditional structures, and that this has entailed dislocation and readjustment for many individuals and groups. However, "For the most part, professionalization was portrayed as a beneficial and virtually inevitable part of an increasingly complex and interdependent world" (Geison 1983: 4). For Parsons, indeed, professionals were seen as the carriers and exemplars of modernity (represented in his "pattern variables"); if experts had become a powerful new elite, such a meritocracy was both fairer and more productive than the power structures it supplanted (cf. also Berger et al. 1974, on the importance of "modernizing elites" and the cultivation of "technological and bureaucratic consciousness" in modernizing societies).

These themes are all manifest in liberal accounts of the emergence of "modern sport." Guttmann (1978) and Adelman (1986) present sophisticated versions of this analysis. They argue that the professionalization of sport – including, crucially, the professionalization of performance, as well as coaching and administration – is an aspect of the emergence of modern societies and is simply an instance of themes discussed above: the application of the scientific world view, the development of a highly specialized division of labour, and the spread of universal standards and aspirations. They acknowledge that modern sport has its problems, but consider that technical and bureaucratic rationalization has made new levels of sporting excellence available to both performers and spectators (cf. Gruneau 1988, for a review and critique of this account of the development of modern sport). This positive stance, arguably, is the Sport Canada view. If it is assessed in its own terms, moreover, there is considerable evidence to support it. Indeed, it is worth noting that Guttmann also argues that these developments are basically democratic. Our own demographic data (cf. Macintosh and Beamish 1988) offer qualified support for the suggestion that if the professionals who now run Canadian sport constitute a new institutional elite, they are more open and merit-ocratic than the upper-middle-class anglophone males who made up the volunteer elite (cf. Hollands and Gruneau 1979). There is evidence in our work that men from working-class backgrounds have achieved substantial representation in administrative and technical positions in high-performance sport, but little evidence of such success by women and francophones. This topic receives more attention in chapter 7.

In contrast, conflict theorists emphasize the importance of conflicts between interest groups and ways of life in the understanding of social change; they maintain that to talk blandly of the "emergence" of new elites and new social formations takes the real people out of struggles in which there have been losers as well as winners. Indeed, the matter-of-fact use of terms like "modernization" and "progress" simply reflects the capacity of dominant groups to put positive constructions on the changes they have effected. Socio-historical analysis that starts from the assump-tions of conflict theorists typically seeks to clarify the processes by which victories are achieved and consolidated. It also seeks to explore the effects of structural changes (e.g., "economic restructuring") at the grass roots upon those whose work-place is radically changed by automation (cf. Garson 1988), or whose way of life is effectively displaced by changes they did not initiate (cf. Berger 1985). Finally, conflict theory allows us to examine what we lose collectively as our environment, our daily rhythms, and our social relationships are steadily transformed in our relentless quest for "progress" (cf. Bellah et al. 1985). In each case, there is a clear sense that social changes involve struggles between different interests (which may involve gender and regional interests as well as class interests), and an awareness that the costs and benefits of progress are usually unevenly distributed.

These are exactly the issues that are emphasized in conflict analyses of professionalization. Certainly, there is evidence that established profes-sions like medicine and law routinely use their monopolies of socially necessary knowledge to advance and defend their own self-interest (cf. Freidson 1970; Starr 1982). Conversely, there are accounts of the efforts of semi-professions and new occupational groups to establish the "profes-sional" nature of their expertise and thereby secure their niche in relation to other allied professions (e.g., chiropractors and nurses, as well as various therapists, in the spectrum of health care professionals). Here, it is possible, although by no means necessary, that the public interest and an aspirant profession's self-interest can coincide. But in any case, it is clear that a "project" of professionalization is being undertaken (cf. Larson 1977), and that one group's gain encroaches to some extent on the privileges of established groups. These tensions were clearly present in the ambitions, as well as the resistance, that surrounded the emergence of sport management professionals in Canadian NSOs.

In our analysis of Sport Canada's changing relationship with the formerly volunteer-structured NSOs, we found Johnson's discussions (1972) of "state patronage" and "state mediation" helpful in clarifying what these struggles were about. In the former case, Johnson suggests, the state creates agencies which provide services (e.g., research services or community development services) that it deems to be in the public good. In the latter, the state subsidizes the provision of professional services to client individuals or groups who could not otherwise afford them; at the same time, however, the state effectively structures the professional-client relationship by defining client needs, and sometimes even the manner in which needs will be served (ibid., 77–9). In either case, professionals and clients alike lose some of their prerogatives to a state, which in paying the piper assumes the right to call at least some of the tunes. Again, Johnson's analysis sheds light on the ambivalence we found in many volunteer executives about staffing developments which promised improved competitive performance. Likewise, it illuminates some of the conflicts some professionals experienced between the demands of consumer (i.e., NSOs) needs and those of administrative (i.e., Sport Canada) policies.

Finally, some conflict theorists draw attention to a conflict that transcends, in its political significance, the conflicts identified above between specific groups of experts, and between emergent professional elites and traditional elites. This conflict stems from what Johnson (1972) describes as the incorporation of professional advisers and experts into the apparatus of government decision making. It is ultimately about the role that experts will play in the formation of policy in many kinds of public institutions (cf. Larson 1984). On the one hand, the application of scientific expertise to public policy issues and the restructuring of policy-making structures so that expert opinion is afforded a greater weight promises more informed policies. On the other hand, conflict theorists worry about how the definition of problems as *requiring* scientific advice and expertise often serves as a reason for rejecting the claims of lay citizens to be heard (Offe 1984). They also are concerned about how the habit of deference to experts is gradually restricting the meaning and effectiveness of our political institutions (Larson 1984). Haskell (1984) summarizes these concerns: "the constantly expanding claims of experts shrink the sphere within which common sense seems adequate, and thereby exclude from political debate a wide range of questions relevant to every citizen's well-being" (ibid., xxii).

III   GROWING CONFLICT

All of the conflicts enunciated above, but especially the general conflict between "experts" (i.e., the professional staff) and the lay public (i.e., the volunteer board members), surfaced in our interviews with key actors in Canadian high-performance sport. To those within the sport community whose primary interest had always been the elite programs, and who had fought running (and often losing) battles with coalitions of provincial interests and others whose concerns were grass-roots development, the federal government's thrust towards high-performance sport in the 1970s provided a welcome reinforcement of their own priorities. Even in this constituency, nonetheless, it was typically felt that the sports themselves knew their own needs. At the same time, however, there were also some within the volunteer community who objected explicitly to the clear push towards high performance, pointing to the lack of comparable support for junior development, for recreational sport, or for the needs of a variety of special groups (e.g., native Canadians and disabled people). One board member stated that "development work is important not just for its ultimate contribution to the high-performance program, but in and of itself." We should note here that this view was sometimes shared by professional staff holding more junior positions in the NSOs, such as domestic program coordinators; however, these staff members were not key actors in their respective NSOs and, therefore, were not part of the formal pool of people that we interviewed.

The government's response to such concerns, as articulated in two successive white papers (Campagnolo 1979; Regan 1981), was to acknowledge them, but to insist that the magnitude of the challenge (i.e., building on the improvements in Canada's international performances already registered in the 1978 Commonwealth Games), together with the financial responsibilities incumbent upon a government, required that the federal government "confirm its commitment" to playing an active role. Government would "work with the national associations in the development of adequate management, accounting and monitoring processes, without interfering with the autonomy of the national associations" (Regan 1981: 7–8).

This, of course, is not unique to sport. Van Til (1985) has pointed out how, as government has provided increasing resources to many kinds of voluntary organizations (and in the process divested some of its own welfare responsibilities onto the voluntary sector), it has also required that they become more businesslike in their conduct of their own affairs. The result has been a new emphasis on management in the voluntary sector, and a push to replace volunteer management with professional management. In sport, monitoring has also meant a regular evaluation of associations' high-performance results, with priority funding promised to those sports able to demonstrate that their programs were producing results. As Macintosh et al. (1987b: 148) comment, this has reinforced the leverage of the Sport Canada bureaucracy in their "work with" the NSOs. Effectively, it has meant that NSOs have had little choice but to put high-performance programs before domestic development. It is noteworthy, however, that by 1987, Sport Canada recognized that this had led in some sports to the neglect of domestic programming. Thus, in the 1988–92 quadrennial planning guide (Fitness and Amateur Sport 1988), NSOs were asked to attend to planning for domestic development as well.

In any case, since the early 1980s, Sport Canada has "worked with" the NSOs in the institution of a monitoring process known as quadrennial planning (a brief history of quadrennial planning forms part of chapter 3). This requires an association to identify performance targets for a four-year period (corresponding to the cycle of major international games) and identify the material and technical support systems (from training camps and "centres of excellence" to coaching and paramedical appointments and research programs) which will need to be in place for each set of targets to be realistic. Without doubt, quadrennial planning has forced organizations to think more systematically about the relationships between the different aspects of a successful high-performance program.

In addition, however, the quadrennial planning process has forced many NSOs to confront the possibility that further technical and competitive development may also require the kinds of organizational development outlined by Hinings and Slack (1987): a bureaucratic rationalization involving a restructuring of lines of authority between professionals and volunteers (and within each group), the end result of which is clearly an organization that will be directed by professionals. It is undoubtedly true that there were significant numbers in the volunteer community (more in some sports than others) who were enthusiastic about such a prospect; they saw in it an opportunity to finally realize the goals they themselves had always had for Canadians in international sport. There were others who were less enthusiastic, but nonetheless accepted professionalization as a necessary evil. Finally, there were those who were unhappy for a variety of reasons, and who expressed different kinds of reservation and even engaged in resistance. We illustrate and explore some of these mixed responses in the next section.

IV   QUADRENNIAL PLANNING: 1984–88

The comments on planning and professionalization which follow are drawn from the interview part of our study (see appendix A for an explanation of the methodology utilized). One of our interests was precisely the effect of professionalization on the relative balance between mass and elite sport programs. In other words, was there a shift in emphasis from the former to the latter which could be attributed to professionalization? Those interviewed were balanced roughly equally between volunteers and professionals; volunteers were represented by current and former board members, and professionals by current and former executive and technical directors and by Sport Canada consultants. We anticipated that their accounts of how specific program policies had been developed would tell us something about the relative influence of professionals and volunteers in the policy development in these organizations, and would also reveal something about how each group now views its own role, and that of the other, in the future of the sport.

It was the issue of mass versus elite sport programs rather than quadrennial planning itself that was an initial focus of the study. However, it quickly became clear that, as Hinings and Slack's work (1987) suggests, this planning process required participants to confront the likelihood of profound changes in organizational structures and in policy-making processes, if technical objectives (and ultimately, performance objectives) were to be achieved. These changes clearly pointed, as Hinings and Slack indicate, to a professionally controlled organization with a lessened, or at least modified, support role for volunteers. It was not surprising, therefore, that it was in the responses to this planning process that feelings about professionalization and attitudes about Sport Canada's promotion of a high-performance mission were most clearly articulated.

Our work suggested that the professional staff that we interviewed were without exception committed both to the high performance mission and to the centrality of their own role in pursuing it. The responses of volunteers ranged from enthusiastic commitment to both high performance and professionalization, through a commitment to high performance but ambivalence about professionalization and a desire to retain the tradition of volunteer control, to ambivalence about the mission as well as defensiveness about professional encroachment and Sport Canada interference.

Exemplifying the first category was one large NSO, where a belief in the benefits of professionalization appeared to be widely shared among the volunteers. This sport had conducted its own strategic planning exercise even before Sport Canada introduced quadrennial planning; this first planning process had sought to reach out widely to the provinces and clubs, and to involve the grass roots in a discussion of ends and roles as well as strategies. "Dropping a penny in the water and letting the ripples spread" was how one key volunteer described the efforts to legitimize the idea of planning for excellence within the sport community. The resulting agreement that the role of the national program was to support the elite in their efforts to be world class has meant a widespread sense of "ownership" of the high-performance "mission statement" which subsequently came out of quadrennial planning. It also meant a more widely shared understanding of why various organizational changes, including professionalization, were deemed to be necessary in order for the sport to achieve the goals it had set itself. Finally, it meant widespread commitment to making these changes work.

In part, this enthusiasm for change appeared to exist in this NSO because there was, in the professional leadership, a strong commitment to the continuing importance of the volunteer in the sport. "We know that volunteers are always going to be the lifeblood of our sport. We need to involve good people, and to run the sport in such a way that good people want to stay involved." This commitment contrasted with the ambition of an executive director in another sport to be "able to deliver program without volunteers." In the first NSO, however, professionals spoke thoughtfully about planning for volunteer development and about restructuring committee processes so that volunteers would find their roles fulfilling, and would be likely to feel that time spent on the sport's committees was time well spent. This NSO, it can be suggested, clearly manifests the positive effects of what Ulrich (1987) has called "transformational leadership."

Considerable attention, indeed, had been devoted to committee memberships and procedures. With respect to membership, it was regarded as an important development that the association's working committees were now built on the basis of skills, i.e., on the kinds of input required, rather than on regional representation. This was seen as utilizing the human resources available to the sport more effectively, even though it also had had a depoliticizing effect which is discussed more fully in the next chapter. Although there were some initiatives in this direction in other sports, this NSO had given more attention to the recruitment and development of volunteers with "appropriate" skills than had any of the other organizations in our study.

The issue of committee information, and of the structuring and scheduling of committee work, however, was seen to be of even greater significance. Indeed, it cut to the heart of professional-volunteer relationships in the management structure. If there were shifts in power or struggles over power, this was where they were disguised or played out. The access of the head office professional to information, and the time (s)he had to devote to it, contrasted with the position of the volunteer, who was often dependent upon summaries and briefing papers prepared by the professional. Indeed, if board members were to participate meaningfully in policy formation, and if they were to oversee the performance of professional staff in the implementation of policy, systems needed to be established whereby board members (and on another level, working committees) were in timely receipt of the kinds of information they needed in order to do their jobs effectively. It is only through such reporting systems that corporate boards can exercise constructive influences (let alone control) over companies; likewise, it is only with the development of such reporting systems that the "corporate-volunteer" model outlined above can really work.

A contrary view was expressed by one professional staff member, now with another sport, who saw the role of NSO boards as much more limited. Rather like members of hospital boards (his comparison), they were not qualified to assess professional competence, let alone participate in program and policy decisions.

The function of boards in public institutions like hospitals, libraries, and in my view NSOs, is to participate in fund raising and public relations campaigns and generally to represent the institution's interests in the community. It is *not* to participate actively in the running of the institution.

This view had not prevailed, however. Volunteer board members were happy with the quality of the information they got, satisfied that policy options were presented fairly and completely and that revised drafts then reflected the board's input. On the professional side, the aspiration was expressed that an organizational structure be created, encompassing professionals and senior volunteers, but also as many clubs as wished to be part of it, in which a "results-orientation" would be exciting and satisfying, in which the development of successors would be an ongoing phenomenon, and in which the structure and its traditions would be strong enough to encompass the expression of different opinions.

It was also suggested in this first NSO that the cultivation of a role for volunteers within the organizational structure needed to be recognized as part of the professional's workload: not just as a separate task (i.e., volunteer development), but rather as something that was integral to the success of all the central program areas (coaching, administration, etc.). This "transformational" leadership in this first NSO contrasted with the other five NSOs in our study; in none of these later five were such things discussed. This finding broadly supports Hinings and Slack's suggestion (1987) that the lack of attention to volunteer development which characterized most NSOs in their work may be a source of future problems (ibid.; 141–2).

In three other sports, the volunteer executives interviewed shared almost unanimously with the professionals a strong commitment to high-performance sport. However, there was markedly less consensus concerning who had what roles in the making and implementation of policy. Many board members saw it as their right, and indeed their job, to be involved in many kinds of program decisions. The professional staff, meanwhile, often complained about "meddling" and about "not being able to do the jobs we are hired to do." The volunteer executives, for the most part, were simply doing what people in their position have always expected to do. The opportunity to exercise such authority may be one reason they had sought office; usually they had achieved election because they were recognized within their respective sports as knowledgeable and energetic individuals.

The professional staff in these three NSOs, however, expressed frustration with the extent to which people who had been builders in the sport at the local and provincial levels either exaggerated their technical knowledge or "failed" to distinguish between the issues on which they had a contribution to make and those where their knowledge was "amateur." It should be pointed out that this argument was a clear instance of a "technocratic" position which, from another perspective, could be said to fail to recognize where decisions made on technical grounds have far-reaching human and organizational implications (cf. Habermas 1971: chap. 6). Decisions about talent identification programs, for example, about psychological testing, or about the role of a national centre or national coach are not simply technical decisions. They might also be the legitimate objects of interest to athletes' representatives, to coaches' representatives, to regional representatives, and to those who might oppose the intensive training of young athletes or the use of psychological testing.

However, it is precisely the notion of democratic checks on technical professionals which, from a technocratic viewpoint, is the source of the problem (cf. Offe 1984: chap. 7). This perspective came out most clearly in criticisms of the quadrennial planning process as an "elaborate charade." "Sport Canada wants to play the democratic game," it was suggested; but when professionals were the ones who knew how to do the job Sport Canada wanted done, the "democratic game" only put barriers in their way. It required them, in turn, to become manipulative: to "plant" ideas, to "politic," etc. When professional staff had board members who could bring specific and complementary kinds of expertise, and who understood their role as an advisory one, the professionals felt they could benefit from this independent source of advice. The professionals held this to be both more honest and more productive than saying to volunteers, "You come up with the program, and we'll run it," when they did not really believe that the volunteers had the knowledge necessary to do this effectively.

It is important to indicate that this viewpoint was also articulated by some volunteers in the NSOs. One such individual suggested that the extent to which some board members second-guessed staff on program decisions, and even the extent to which Sport Canada was concerned with democracy and "grass-roots ownership" of policy, were each evidence in their own way that "Canadians pay lip service to excellence, but aren't willing to pay the price" when that price involves sacrifices in democratic participation and due process. This viewpoint is represented here because it presents in a clear form one of the options for Canadian sport: a path which is frankly elitist (or proudly and single-mindedly dedicated to excellence), in which "results-oriented" professionals who are judged on their results would run the program, and in which the role of the volunteer would be largely that of fund-raiser. Indeed, the individual cited above also suggested that the eligibility requirement for directors should be the ability to open corporate doors. In such a structure, as Habermas's analysis (1971) would predict, the effect of democratic process on decisions determined by technical imperatives would be very much reduced. Clearly, the assumption is that this more streamlined and results-oriented structure would produce the desired outcomes; equally clearly, it would profoundly alter both the management and the governance of Canadian high-performance sport.

A very different and more traditional scenario is pointed to in the struggles that continued to rock the final NSO we shall consider here. In this NSO, opposition to professionalization could not be extricated from misgivings about Sport Canada's imposition of a high-performance mandate on the sport. Everyone in the sport was proud of the national teams and wanted to build on their successes. Yet several directors expressed concern that grass-roots development should not be ignored and that the national association should continue to serve the needs of club- and school-level coaches and officials. There was also considerable resistance to proposals, which had emanated from the quadrennial planning exercise, that the association appoint a high-performance director and that the executive director be upgraded to a director-general, both positions which in the Sport Canada structure were intended to carry operational autonomy.

There was widespread agreement in this final NSO that quadrennial planning had been a worthwhile experience in that it had been a catalyst to people in the sport in clarifying the different support structures on which successful national teams depend. However, there were board members who felt that it had been a rigged process, in which the steering committee – composed of Sport Canada representatives, professional staff, and board members selected because they favoured a greater high-performance focus – had solicited input primarily from others whose priorities were the same as their own. The steering committee had only discussed *how* high performance could be accomplished more effectively; it had not seriously considered options that started from premises *different* from this presupposed system goal.

Whether or not the planning process was manipulated in this final NSO to produce the results Sport Canada wanted, it is fair to say that there was sufficient resistance to its conclusions (or sufficiently little "ownership," in the Sport Canada parlance) that the job of the new high-performance director was rendered very difficult. Board members continued to question program decisions and to request so much background information that much of the time of senior professionals was absorbed in justifying themselves. Board members were within their constitutional rights here, but their behaviour was a retreat from the commitment supposedly agreed to in this organization's quadrennial plan. Instinctively, resistance was also expressed by a board member in the observation that "If Sport Canada wants professionals to run the high-profile Olympic sports, why don't they simply insist on this, and not waste people's time on planning exercises designed to produce this result and no other?"

However, it can be suggested that quadrennial planning was intended to produce two kinds of results. At a manifest level, as Hinings and Slack observe (1987), it is "designed to produce change by requiring sport organizations to rethink their goals and objectives and introduce new organizational structures and processes" (ibid., 129). However, on another level, it was also intended to prepare the ground for a qualitative, and arguably irreversible, shift in the direction of professionalization, by requiring the volunteers' participation in a process designed to secure their own recognition and agreement that "better results in the high performance sport area is ... at least partially dependent on the existence of a rational, professionally organized and controlled management system" (ibid., 141). Through participation in quadrennial planning, volunteers were expected to realize the need for their own demise, or at least a radical change in their roles in these sport organizations, if their own goals were to be accomplished. The planning process, in other words, was intended to produce a wider commitment to these changes than if Sport Canada had simply imposed them. As Hinings and Slack add (ibid.), organizations do not plan if their goal is simply to remain the same. Planning starts from a commitment to change, and if it is successful, it diffuses that commitment throughout the organization.

Clearly, however, our own data suggest that the results have been uneven. This is supported by the finding of Hinings and Slack (ibid., 142) that NSOs in the mid-1980s were in markedly different "stages" of professionalization, with nineteen of the thirty-six NSOs they studied "neither in the bureaucratic category nor nascently moving toward it." In at least one of the NSOs we studied, planning had had precisely the effects intended. It had provided a blueprint for fundamental organizational change (i.e., to a new, "corporate-volunteer" structure). In addition, it had also facilitated an understanding of the reasons for change, at many different levels of the organization, and a widely shared commitment to making the new structures work. The other associations we studied, however, suggested that both people who were fully committed to the high-performance mission and those who opposed it could still share strong reservations about the organizational changes which it appeared to require, and about a planning process which had underlined the supposed need for these changes.

It has been observed in other planning contexts that forms of public participation can be deployed to lend a spurious democratic legitimacy to rational planning processes that, in reality, have ruled out in advance any questions or solutions that cannot be accommodated within presupposed system goals (Kemp 1985; Forester 1985). When this is being done, or even when it is widely perceived that it is being done, Kemp suggests, resentment about outcomes can be augmented by resentment at time wasted in a process that was not genuine, in the sense that the outcome was never in doubt. From the professional side, conversely, there are resentments at time wasted in politicking, rather than used in getting on with a task that is, in their view, of self-evident urgency.

Quadrennial planning, it is proposed here, illustrates all of these phenomena. In contrast to the "strategic planning" in the successful association (the first NSO), which allowed for debate about ends as well as means, the presupposed system goal in quadrennial planning was perceived to be the preparation of the high-performance athlete. The object of planning was simply to clarify better ways of achieving this goal. When people could criticize it from *both* sides as an "elaborate charade," however, as "playing the democratic game," it was clear that, in at least half of the NSOs we studied, some of the important participants felt the resentments described above.

V   DISCUSSION

In our view, the dynamics described here raise several questions, first, about quadrennial planning, but ultimately about the impact of the advent of professional management and sport sciences on democracy in Canadian sport. In the first instance, we simply want to argue that quadrennial planning offers clear illustrations of the problems raised by Forester (1985) and Kemp (1985), i.e., that we need to ask of any public participation process whether it honestly seeks to be a catalyst for citizen input into planning, or whether it is intended simply to assist in the ratification of a solution already decided upon.

With respect to the broader issues, several phenomena are worth comment. First, it is clear that professionals' *power* is augmented at the same time that their *autonomy* is constrained in their work situations, situations which Johnson (1972) suggests are characterized by corporate and state patronage. Professionals who work for large corporations and government find that their impact in the world is enhanced by the fact that they exercise their knowledge as representatives of economically and/or politically powerful institutions. This is to say little more than that many intellectuals have found it easier to influence events from within the system. However, it is also to recognize that their role as representatives of government affords them powers (e.g., to approve or deny resources) that do not normally attach to the independent professional.

At the same time, working within a government or corporate bureaucracy imposes its own constraints; certainly, the ideal of professional autonomy, or "freedom to exercise judgement in respect to work objectives and processes" (Freidson 1984), is very much constrained by the interests and hierarchical structures of the institutions these professionals represent. Instead of offering diagnoses and prescribing solutions as independent consultants to clients who need them more than they need the clients, these professionals are employees working on the problems of their employers, and they must address these problems from a corporate or departmental point of view. Often, moreover as Johnson (1972) points out, their solutions become common or standardized solutions (whether these mean standard designs of apartment blocks, standardized reading curricula, or quadrennial planning models). These standard solutions are then implemented in a variety of contexts in which needs are defined as similar, even though clients may feel their circumstances are unique. This was illustrated in several accounts of quadrennial planning, where despite some efforts by Sport Canada consultants to tailor the process to the realities of a given sport, the clients expressed resentment that models had been imposed which did not take account of their own uniqueness.

These tensions are further complicated in the situation Johnson (ibid.) calls "mediative control," where state policies structure the relationships between nominally independent professionals and clients by defining what services will be publicly funded, by setting financial limits, and sometimes by supervision. Mediative control can be as powerful as that exercised by senior governments over relations between local school boards and teachers, or as loose as consumer protection legislation which affords complaint mechanisms outside professional peer-review bodies. Sport professionals working for NSOs are arguably closer to the former, given that they are hired with Sport Canada funding, according to (increasingly standard) job descriptions approved by Sport Canada. The result is that even their own staff members are seen by some volunteer executives as representatives of the Sport Canada view. Indeed, some professionals clearly see themselves as part of trends in Canadian sport that are actively promoted by Sport Canada, but that enjoy only grudging acceptance among some of the volunteer executives in their own sport.

The point we wish to raise, first of all, is that the circumstances of professional work are altered in fundamental ways by the growth of professional bureaucracies. And it is not that professionals working in these less than autonomous situations are any less professional than independent entrepreneurs; instead, we need to understand that the rationalization of public administration (as well as many kinds of knowledge-dependent corporate enterprises) and the increasing presence of government intervention and mediation in many areas of society lead almost inevitably to the incorporation of experts into government (Ingham 1975). What is indisputable is that the negotiation of the role of sport management experts, especially in the mediated instance represented by the NSO, takes place against a background of complications and very difficult issues.

The first complication has been alluded to above, and tends to be understood simply as a matter of divided loyalties, or of professionals' identification with a Sport Canada perspective that authorizes a more important role for people like themselves in Canadian sport. The background reality, however, is that public service professionals are always, as Johnson (1972) suggests, in the difficult position of mediating between clients' perceptions of their needs, their own "professional" perceptions of these needs, and the state's definition of these needs (constrained as this inevitably is by political, administrative, and financial objectives). Individual practitioners may, as Johnson suggests (ibid., 81), become personally committed either to client or to administrative perspectives. The tensions do not disappear, however, because they are grounded ultimately in different views about the proper role of government in civil society and the objectives of government intervention in different social institutions. It is important, therefore, for us to comprehend how professionals are encouraged to understand the role *of* government, as well as their own role *in* government; do they have a responsibility as public servants to work for equity and democracy, or is their function a more narrowly technical or administrative one?

The second complication follows from the way in which the professional understands his/her role; it concerns the implications of the growing role of experts in the making of policy in many kinds of public institutions. From the functionalist perspective, this is desirable for society. The removal of important policy areas (especially economic policy) to a sphere where the best policies can be determined by experts, and where the policy process can be insulated from political trade-offs and from democratic pressures, is even deemed essential (Crozier et al. 1976). It represents the "end of ideology" (Bell 1976) and the triumph of "cognitive rationality" (Parsons 1954).

In sport, this functionalist line of thinking is manifest in arguments that the professionalization of policy making means an end to national team policies being decided in a context of inter-provincial bargaining, and that policies that involve complex technical and financial issues can no longer be left to "well-meaning schoolteachers" (or housewives or firemen). All these occupations and others were cited by professionals whom we interviewed as examples of volunteer executives' unsuitability for important policy roles. Thus, the creation of new forms of expertise, through the application of science and social science to successive areas of life, is presented not only as self-justifying (because of the superior results it produces), but as justifying the ascendancy of new groups of experts and the depoliticization of successive social institutions (cf. Habermas 1971; Offe 1984). Indeed, Balbus (1975) suggests that when the authority of experts is successfully modelled on that of the airline pilot, democratic participation can be represented as not only unnecessary but potentially harmful (ibid., 326–8).

One does not have to pretend, however, that democratic decisions are always wise, or that they are not time-consuming, in order to suggest that important issues are obscured by those who propose that policy making be the responsibility of experts. The first of these is the tendency of experts, noted by Habermas and Offe, to see the production of results as a technical challenge. This leads to solutions that involve new work (or training) processes, for example, or new levels of bureaucratic rationalization, being presented as purely technical issues. Such solutions usually, of course, require new behaviours of people or require new organizational structures, either of which may have ethical or political implications. They may simply entail human costs for the practitioners (e.g., enjoyment of one's sport or moving to another community) that are difficult if not impossible to calculate in any technical sense. The effect, in any case, is that other issues are subordinated to the pursuit of technical possibilities, at the same time that the representation of planning processes as involving essentially technical issues serves to limit the claims of non-experts (even those who are directly affected) to a say in these processes.

In conclusion, it is important to acknowledge that the federal and provincial sport bureaucracies have produced degrees of administrative and technical competence that were undreamt of in the 1960s, and this will very likely be reflected in successful performances by Canadian athletes in future international events. However, the corollary of this technical progress has been a tendency to subordinate political and ethical questions – questions relating to the commitment of government to addressing gender, class, and regional inequities, for instance – to the pursuit of high-performance goals. A further corollary has been a restructuring of policy-making bodies; the effect (if not necessarily the intention) of this restructuring has been to reduce the likelihood of politically representative input that could challenge the technical/rational framework within which policy is increasingly made. For our research suggests that there are Canadians, even at the upper level of NSOs, who want to maintain a place for other meanings and values and practices than those associated with the rationalized production of performance. There are others, moreover, who have been excluded from decision-making circles, or have dropped out themselves because of the apparent futility of raising issues that were routinely dismissed as "irrelevant" from the perspective of this rational discourse. We are reminded here of Offe's observation (1984) that historical evidence suggests that the participation of experts in successive areas of policy serves the function of rejecting the claims of lay citizens to be heard.

Freidson's perspective (1984) on this trend is instructive: "Only part of any kind of work is technical, based on truly esoteric knowledge and skill; ... In order to put technical knowledge and skill into practice one must establish social and moral relationships with those involved in its application, lay and otherwise" (ibid., 24). Freidson considers that expertise is necessary in a modern society, and that there are issues or aspects of issues on which we must defer to experts. However, if we want to enjoy the fruits of expertise without undermining the fundamentals of a democratic society, it is important for professionals and lay people alike to be able to distinguish the parts of any issue that are technical from those that have social and political and moral implications. It is also important to preserve policy-making structures in which these political and moral questions remain open to political representations and in which, ultimately, decisions are made by lay persons with the benefit of expert advice.

Forester (1985) suggests that many kinds of experts in our society have promoted "the political and moral illusion that science and technology, through professionals and experts, can solve problems" which are, at bottom, political and ethical problems (ibid., 205). However, if democracy is to refer not simply to a system of government but to a society in which citizens communicate together in order to decide how they want to live (Macpherson 1973), it will be necessary to strengthen the capacity of lay people to challenge such claims and to broaden the parameters within which policy is made. This is all the more necessary in light of the issues raised by the Dubin inquiry into the use of drugs in Canadian high-performance sport. In the ensuing chapters, we seek to illustrate these points in discussions of several issues concerning the distribution of opportunities in sport in Canada, issues which we found were often submerged and even denied in increasingly "professional" discussions of how best to accomplish the high-performance mission.

CHAPTER FIVE

Rational Planning vs Regional Interests

I INTRODUCTION

The role assumed by the federal government in the promotion of Canadian high-performance sport offers an interesting, and sometimes contradictory, illustration of the tensions between a centralist rationality and regional interests in Canadian social planning. We argue in this chapter that the organizational changes being promoted by Sport Canada in the name of high-performance sport – a technical and bureaucratic structure, whose key features are professionalization and centralization – are changes whose effect is a further concentration of resources in metropolitan areas of Canada which are already relatively privileged. They are, moreover, changes that render it increasingly difficult for representatives of those regions which stand to suffer most to mount any effective opposition to a withdrawal from a domestic development role on the part of national sport organizations (NSOs). We argue further that what is typically framed by proponents of high-performance sport as a choice between rational planning and "kitchen table" amateurism, the national interest and provincialism, high-performance and embarrassing mediocrity – the good guys and the dinosaurs – can from another perspective be seen as a campaign by federal and professional interests to redefine what is really a redirection of resources and an appropriation of policy prerogatives.

First, we make some brief observations on regional distributions of high-performance athletes in Canada and on the likely effects of the centralization of programs which require national teams to train together for team sports and encourage individual sport athletes to relocate to centralized national and regional training centres, referred to as centres of excellence. Second, we attend to efforts to restructure volunteer boards of directors in a variety of ways which weaken the relative strength of regional representation. Third, we consider arguments which suggest that the world view of professional sport staff is often oriented nationally and internationally, both by the structures of their own careers and by discourses which emphasize abstract standards of excellence over commitments to real individuals and communities. The concluding section seeks to connect the phenomena described above with tendencies familiar in "core-periphery" relations and to situate centralist/regional tensions in Canadian sport in the context of broader struggles between different conceptions of the purposes of Canadian social policy.

All the professional staff members whom we interviewed were based in Ottawa and were employees or former employees of either the NSO concerned or Sport Canada. As project funding did not support travel outside central Canada, most of our volunteer sources were also based there. However, we were able, in two sports (track and field and basketball), to meet with volunteers from other regions who were in Ontario to attend NSO meetings; in two others (volleyball and swimming), we were able to conduct telephone interviews with individuals who had played important roles. Regionalism was not initially intended to be a focus of our study. However, the unexpected discovery of an opposition to the high-performance "mission" that was explicitly rooted in regional concerns, combined with the tendency of most professionals and many metropolitan (especially Ontario-based) volunteers to dismiss such opposition as "provincialism," together led us to consider that there were issues here worth pursuing.

II   REGIONAL BENEFITS FROM ELITE SPORT SPENDING

Background data on the regional bases of those Canadian athletes who received support from Sport Canada's Athlete Assistance Program (AAP) illustrate the degree of centralization of training opportunities for high-performance athletes. These data, collected by Macintosh and Albinson (1985) in 1984–85, indicated that when location of training was related to size of community, 84 per cent of AAP athletes were located in large urban centres (over 100,000 population), while only 3 per cent were located in small town or rural environments (under 20,000). These figures refer to where the athlete was training rather than to community of origin; further research would be needed to demonstrate that athletes who grew up in particular parts of the country stand to benefit disproportionately from policies that channel federal monies into national team-related programs rather than into domestic development.

Nonetheless, there is some evidence that high-performance athletes in individual sports tend to be the products of large urban and suburban clubs, who can hire elite coaches as well as development coaches. There are exceptions, of course, especially in those sports where climate or terrain is an important factor. In the sports we studied, however, this pattern held. It was most pronounced in those sports where clubs hired professional coaches; thus, swimming and gymnastics were dominated by athletes from elite clubs: in Etobicoke, Pointe Claire, and Calgary, for swimming; in Oshawa and elsewhere in the "Golden Horseshoe" for gymnastics. In sports where professional coaching was less established, or even events where technical coaching was less necessary (e.g., middle distance running), there were more exceptions. Nonetheless, track remained dominated by the big clubs from Metro Toronto (e.g., Scarborough Optimists) and the Vancouver area and canoeing by athletes based in Ottawa and Mississauga. Figures from the 1988 *Canadian Track and Field Association Handbook* confirmed this. If one allots immigrants from the Caribbean and Europe to the Canadian cities they moved to, only 11 of 130 national team members came from the six smallest provinces, while only 9 of 130 came from towns with populations under 100,000.

In team sports, the club system was less important than the high schools in the process of player development, so that differentials in community resources were to some extent ameliorated. However, the ready availability of good quality competition remained important, so that elite basketball players, for example, were more likely to emerge from the very competitive high school leagues of southern Ontario and greater Vancouver than elsewhere.

Such differences as already existed were sharpened, moreover, by the centralization of national teams and the support of centres of excellence through Sport Canada funds. Centralization of a team must necessarily take into account the needs of these high-performance athletes to have career and/or educational opportunities available to them; this typically favoured those cities (Toronto, Montreal, Vancouver) that could offer a range of opportunities in either area. A further bias towards Toronto and Montreal (and Ottawa) was constituted by travel costs, and, in the view of one sport administrator, by the difficulties of maintaining financial controls over an operation that was taking place far from the supervision of the national office.

An exception in the NSOs we studied was the women's volleyball team, which had been located in Regina for several years. This was in part due to the efforts of a Saskatchewan-based executive committee member and to the willingness of the city to offer some inducements. The executive committee felt that the team benefited from greater civic and media interest than the sport could likely attract in a larger centre. However, there were apparently complaints from players, especially francophones, about the lack of opportunities for them outside the sport.

The centres of excellence were usually established and maintained through a negotiated arrangement between the NSO, Sport Canada, a university (which provides facilities and sport science support), and a provincial government. The Universities of Calgary, Victoria, and Western Ontario had broken the big city monopoly here. The location of these exceptions only served to underline, however, that where federal (i.e., Sport Canada) funding is dependent upon a commitment of complementary funds by a province, this funding will only go to those provinces that are able and willing to put funds into high-performance sport themselves.

This, in turn, points to the final issue we want to raise in this section, which is differences in the capacity of provincial governments to mount serious grass-roots development programs in a range of sports. The problem, of course, is that while Ontario and Quebec have established their own sport bureaucracies to support most of the Olympic sports, and Alberta, British Columbia, and Saskatchewan have committed themselves to more focused but still substantial support for provincial sport associations, the rest of the provinces have not been able or willing to do so. New Brunswick is typical of the Maritime pattern, with only a handful of provincial sport organizations with part-time executive directors. Therefore, a withdrawal by the NSOs from the development-oriented services they have historically provided to clubs and schools can only widen existing regional disparities with respect to facilities and coaching, as the richer and more populous provinces pull further ahead. It is missing the point, in these circumstances, for NSOs and Sport Canada consultants to portray (as they regularly did) representatives from the smaller provinces as parochial, or as not understanding the needs of high-performance sport.

Instead, as one gymnastics respondent put it, "the debate about philosophy is also a debate about resources." In this debate, representatives of the "have not" provinces urged that it was the job of the national program to provide the developmental services (like coaching development clinics) which alone would enable them to upgrade gymnastics in these parts of the country. Meanwhile, representatives from the regions in which these services were being provided by provincial programs said that it was the job of the national program to provide the enriched support for elite gymnasts and coaches (and to generate the funds for these supports) which were necessary if Canadian gymnasts were to succeed internationally. This, of course, was not a struggle unique to gymnastics. It was suggested by several respondents that Canadian sport was caught in a difficult structural situation in which discrepancies in regional development were a fact of life; but the provincially representative structure of most NSO boards of directors has meant that they have been simply another site on which regional interests were fought out.

III   VOLUNTEER RESTRUCTURING

The effects of these regular political struggles were seen as problematic, however, by many NSO professional staff members and Sport Canada consultants. From their perspective, it was self-evident that the *national* program must focus its resources and energies on developing a support system for the elite if international success was to be achieved and sustained. They wanted board members and national committee members who were prepared to take a national perspective and to put the interests of the national program before what were described as "pork-barrel concerns," such as getting a clinic or a tournament for their home province, or fighting for provincial representatives on national teams. They were impatient with what they considered provincialism; yet, they saw it as an endemic problem for Canadian sport, so long as boards of directors were made up of provincial representatives who had to answer to their own constituencies back home.

The professional staff's desire for board members with a national team focus found support, in some sports, from those provinces that placed the most members on national teams. There were suggestions in gymnastics, for example, that board representation be weighted in favour of those regions (one way of getting around equal representation for Ontario and Prince Edward Island) that provided most of the gymnasts and most of the funds. This agenda was strongly opposed, of course, by representatives of smaller provinces, who felt that they must fight to maintain the principle of provincial representation even on working committees. They fought for this, of course, because they believed their interests, which they accepted as different from those of the larger and richer provinces, would be systematically ignored if they were not represented. For instance, Manitoba and Saskatchewan each recorded their dissatisfaction at the quadrennial planning process in women's gymnastics. They contested the result – a reorganization of the professional staff which included firing a national coach who had put much time into conducting grass-roots development clinics; they also argued that the quadrennial planning steering committee had not consulted them before making a recommendation it knew they would oppose. Yet, to the extent that regional interests were fought out in every committee, it became difficult to address challenges that were national in scale.

More radical, however, than the notion of regional (i.e., rather than provincial) representation was a board on which clubs would have a significant level of direct representation. The pressure towards this came primarily in those sports where clubs hired professional coaches (i.e., swimming and gymnastics), who themselves wanted an influence within the national program commensurate with their placement of athletes on national teams. The effect of this, of course, would be to weight boards (and committees) with members from the metropolitan areas, who could be expected to side with their provincial colleagues (indeed, its typical effect would be to multiply representation from the large provinces) in support of high-performance programming and against the diversion of resources into development. Gymnastics has not yet adopted this (although it was advocated by one professional staff member as a way of achieving a more "effective" board). However, swimming had places on its board for the three top performing clubs across the country plus three other clubs.

A development which was underway in almost all sports, however, and which was actively encouraged by Sport Canada, was the appointment of members-at-large, selected for the specific expertise (usually financial or marketing expertise) that they could contribute to the sport. Such skills were undoubtedly necessary in NSOs, the more so, it should be noted, since the Conservative government of the late 1980s was pressing NSOs to raise increasing portions of their budgets from the private sector. In several sports, moreover, the appointment of appropriate individuals to committees, as well as to boards of directors, was seen as an essential component in volunteer development, as well as a way of bringing needed skills into the sport.

The Canadian Track and Field Association (CTFA) was by no means the only NSO to appoint members-at-large; but it had thought more explicitly than most about what experiences would keep good volunteers in the sport or, conversely, turn them away. Considerable attention had been given to making committee work satisfying and to constructing committees so as to offer a "career" within the sport to committed and able volunteers. To this end, it was regarded as an important step that CTFA working committees had recently been put together by appointment, on the basis of the skills required. It was part of a larger strategy to develop and utilize human resources more effectively than regional representation typically permitted.

Despite these clearly enlightened objectives, and despite the manifest good sense, from many perspectives, of appointing members-at-large on the basis of expertise, it was clear that another effect (and sometimes another objective) of such a policy was to increase the presence of those who could be expected to take a national perspective on committees and on boards. Indeed, the CTFA explicitly saw it as important to encourage volunteers to identify with the national program (rather than see themselves as representing the interests of their home province) and to encourage a national perspective on all working committees. From a perspective which took it for granted that the job of NSOs was to produce successful international teams, such a restructuring of the work of volunteers was clearly a positive step, indeed a necessary dimension of organizational change (cf. Hinings and Slack 1987).

It is worth observing, however, that the presence on boards of members-at-large, who shared these assumptions about an NSO's raison d'être, was again (like the election of elite club representatives) a development that was likely to further diminish the voice of those who were fighting for the interests of the poorer regions. Such a move towards depoliticizing planning and program decisions by structuring committees on the basis of expertise rather than regional representation does promise a greater consensus in the pursuit of "presupposed system goals" (Habermas 1971: chaps. 4 and 5). However, it also effectively diminishes the possibility of questioning that consensus. As Offe (1984: chap. 6) has pointed out, to the extent that planning can be portrayed as a technical process, requiring specialist forms of expertise, the impact of politically based opposition, and indeed of democratic processes, can be effectively circumscribed.

Swimming Canada Natation's (SCN) suggestion that success in the international competitive environment required a division of labour within Canadian sport, in which the NSOs concentrated their resources on the elite while the provinces assumed responsibility for grass-roots development, stands as a clear statement of one kind of model for the future of Canadian sport. If this were indeed the future all Canadians wanted, it would be difficult to take issue with the argument that when NSO boards and committees are composed of members who are there as representatives of provinces (some of them small and underdeveloped), Canadian sport is hamstrung by having to appease regional interests. In the context of regional inequality in Canada, however, it is necessary to remind ourselves that to leave development work to the provinces is going to mean that it will take place in the "have" provinces (and regions of provinces, for as one respondent observed, northern Ontario is no better served than New Brunswick). Meanwhile, the peripheral regions of Canada will fall further behind, and will get little or nothing of the monies the Canadian government spends on sport.

IV PROFESSIONALS, RATIONAL PLANNING, AND REGIONAL NEEDS

Those who raised the regional concerns presented in the previous section, or those who simply argued that NSOs should be involved in development activities, were often portrayed by NSO and Sport Canada professionals (as well as by volunteers who identified uncritically with the high-performance mission) as living evidence of the outdated mind-set that has stood in the way of Canada's success in international sport. In this section, we argue that these sport professionals' endeavours to substitute rational planning for political structures of decision-making, and likewise their orientation towards abstract and international (as opposed to concrete and community-based) standards of achievement, are themselves rooted in the world view and life experience of the mobile, often middle-class, professional (cf. Bledstein 1976; Larson 1977).

The world of the sport administrator and the high-performance technical director is not one in which the pull of community figures strongly. This is a pull which keeps many Canadians living in small towns and hinterlands, and which orients many others (even in urban areas) towards kinds of public involvement whose focus is the improvement of community life. However, the skills and the goals of these professional staff members are of a sort that, like those of many other professionals, "typically requires resources that can only be provided by large-scale organizations and commits one to a career path that entails moving from job to job and place to place. A professional must be ready to move to wherever the best opportunities for professional advancement open up" (Bellah et al. 1985: 186). On an interpersonal level, moreover, one's reference groups come to be others involved in the same project. In the National Sport and Recreation Centre (NSRC), professional staff members have coffee and lunch with other technical, executive, and program directors; they are compared, formally as well as informally, to these colleagues. As Bellah puts it: "For such professionals, the experience of community is not primarily local, and their sense of citizenship is not linked to a city or town. Their outlook is cosmopolitan, shaped by higher education and linked to others of similar training and skills ... often widely dispersed geographically" (ibid., 210).

On a more concrete level, the construction of loyalties to the projects of Sport Canada (if not necessarily to Sport Canada itself), observed by Macintosh et al. (1987b), cannot be disconnected from the career structure available to professional staff members in the NSRC. In Canadian sport, career opportunities, and indeed, opportunities to make a difference, mean senior posts in NSOs or in Sport Canada. Such a career choice, of course, means working in Ottawa. Therefore, it is fair to say that most of those who progress in this world identify with the national program (with "Game Plan," with "Best Ever," and ultimately, with the high-performance objectives of Sport Canada) rather than with regions of origin.

Another factor in this identification with national programs is the considerable amount of job mobility within the NSRC (i.e., to jobs with larger, higher-budget NSOs), and between the NSRC and Sport Canada. Data from the questionnaire survey of our study indicated that 75 per cent of the administrative and technical personnel who responded had held two or more jobs in the sport bureaucracy, and 40 per cent had held three or more such jobs. During the course of our study, moreover, within the six NSOs we studied, one high-performance director took up a position with Sport Canada (whence he had come to the NSO), and another Sport Canada consultant moved to the top position in a large NSO, having previously held a more junior position in a different NSO. Several other interviewees had made similar moves within a recent time frame. These career patterns, it can be argued, offer some indication of the extent to which "domain assumptions" are shared by NSO and Sport Canada professionals. They can also be read as indicative of the "cadre spirit" which characterizes this Ottawa-based community of professionals and of the ways in which loyalties are constructed towards *Canadian* sport, rather than to a particular sport, let alone a region.

It is worth commenting briefly on the reconstruction of the meanings of profession and professionalism that are revealed here. Bellah et al. (1985) observe that "*Profession* [emphasis in original text] is an old word, but it took on new meanings when it was disconnected from the idea of a 'calling' and came to express the new conception of a career. ... The profession as career was no longer oriented to any face-to-face community but to impersonal standards of excellence, operating in the context of a national occupational system" (ibid., 119–20). Similarly, Bledstein (1976) has argued, in his analysis of how emergent professions convince the public (and themselves) of the significance of their specialist knowledge, that idealism and self-interest come together in the discourse which now surrounds career. In this concept of career, he suggests that the pursuit of influence by professionals is articulated with the notion of public service, in a language of the profession's contribution to universal ends. In the case of the new sport management professional, these ends are high-performance sport, Canada, and knowledge itself (i.e., sport sciences).

What this analysis suggests is that it is not surprising that the professional staff in NSOs in Ottawa have been in the forefront of moves to impose a centralized and technical orientation on the Canadian sport bureaucracy. Neither is it surprising that they have been active agents in a reorientation of the objectives and programs of Canadian NSOs, a process that has directed these organizations more to the international competitive environment and less towards the servicing of local and regional needs. This orientation, which is captured in the view expressed by one senior sport administrator that NSOs were responsible not to their memberships but to Sport Canada, can be seen as evidence of Bellah et al.'s contention (1985) that for many highly educated professionals, a national or international outlook, like a positive perspective on the benefits of rationalization, is simply taken for granted (ibid., 210). We can see in this new generation of sport scientists and sport managers the successors of earlier generations of Canadian scientists who articulated their own professional projects with the project and the discourse of nation-building (cf. Zeller 1988).

V   CONCLUSIONS

We offer some tentative conclusions about the ambiguities embodied in the centralist policies of the national sport bureaucracy discussed in the previous section in the context of Canadian federalism. Macintosh et al.'s analysis (1987b) of the political processes and policy documents which prepared the ground for the Sport Canada we know today clearly supports an argument that the construction of a visible federal presence in high-performance sport can be seen as consistent with what Milne (1986) characterizes as the Trudeau government's preoccupations with strengthening the federal state, and with using that state wherever possible to strengthen a sense of *Canadian*, as opposed to regional, identity (cf. also Banting 1987). Indeed, because a federal state "must reach out for the emotional support of nationalism to sustain itself" (Milne 1986: 31), it can be suggested that international sport has offered a ready symbol for the nationalist sentiments with which these federal governments have wished to identify their project.

We argue, indeed, that there are important parallels to be recognized between the vigorous role played by the universities and the Canadian

scientific elite in the expansion of the federal government's role in higher
education and research (cf. Axelrod 1982; Milne 1986), the role of the
sport elites (and indeed university physical education departments) circa
1970 in advocating a multi-dimensional federal commitment to high-
performance sport (cf. Macintosh et al. 1987b), and the role, evident in
our own study, of centrally located sport professionals' powerful commitment to what they see as the self-evident value of "the national program."
In Milne's view, a key feature of the "federal state building project"
pursued by the Trudeau governments lay precisely in their ability to
articulate this project with the projects of appropriate coalitions of "progressive" elites and interest groups.

Yet, the irony in this case is that the effect of Sport Canada's vigorous
pursuit of technical and bureaucratic rationalization in Canadian sport
has run counter to the commitment to regional assistance which has been
another foundation of Liberal, and indeed Canadian, social policy. The
Canadian antidote to regional disparities has been to counter the market's
tendencies to push people from peripheral regions to the centres of
population. Through transfer payments, regional development assistance, and public subsidies to cultural institutions (ranging from the CBC
to regional theatre companies and publishing houses), Canadian social
policy has sought to make life on the periphery viable and make opportunities for cultural participation available across the country (cf. Banting
1987; Milne 1986). Indeed, Kidd (1981) has argued that this is, in part,
the context in which the Canadian government has taken a more interventionist role in support of sport than has that of the United States.

Today, however, the consensus which has supported regional policies
is under attack from a coalition of interests which stresses the demands
of international competition. In this discourse, it is argued that support
for the weak (including regional assistance programs) has the effect of
undercutting the capacity of our fittest and most successful representatives
to compete abroad (cf. Courchene 1978). Against this, opponents of free
trade have sought to shift the parameters of the debate, arguing that what
is being presented as simply an economic measure will have profound
and far-reaching effects on Canadian life (cf. Lapierre 1987). It can be
argued that programs which have supported sport development in rural
Canada have been representative of a Canadian public philosophy –
now under threat – in which the demands of international competition
are mitigated by concerns for other ingredients upon which our individual
and collective well-being depends, the viability of communities and
regions in which people have long roots being not least among these.
The crux of the problem, in sport as elsewhere, is the balance to be struck

between expenditures designed to support a Canadian elite in their quest for "world class" levels of excellence, and expenditures designed to provide development opportunities to people in the hinterlands (we use the term "hinterland" here to refer not only to people who are geographically isolated, but to people who, because of their gender or socioeconomic class or ethnic background, do not have access to high-performance sport programs).

One swimming administrator we interviewed argued that if SCN was to be able to deliver the necessary support to existing and potential world class swimmers, it would have to devote all its material and human resources to this task, and cease or curtail the services it has historically provided to development-oriented clubs. He recognized, of course, that clinics, coaching education, and packaged materials for club coaches and administrators were all necessary if the base was to keep producing potential stars. He argued, however, for a division of responsibility in which SCN's role was to work with the elite, while the provinces assumed responsibility for the enrichment of the sport at the grass roots.

This argument, of course, is not dissimilar to the universities' position, noted above, that the national interest requires that the federal government take a leadership role in higher education and research while the provinces maintain their traditional responsibility for mass education. In the contemporary version of this argument, Canadian universities with "world class" aspirations – again, the elite metropolitan universities – argue for a greater share of national (and provincial) expenditures on education. The corollary of more support for these elite, graduate program and research-oriented universities, of course, is less for undergraduate programs, and especially less for the "regional" universities. Yet it is widely believed that there is more than self-interest – although there is clearly that, too – in the claim that only a policy of nationally coordinated support of excellence can enable Canadian scholarship to keep up internationally.

The issues surrounding free trade and higher education are, of course, more complex and far-reaching in their effects on Canadian life than arguments surrounding high-performance sport. The evidence to date suggests, however, that the likely effects of policies whose primary orientation is towards the international competitive environment will include a gradual shift of resources away from "have not" regions and into the already well served metropolitan areas; a gradual reconstruction of policymaking structures so that democratic representation of regional interests is supplanted by "rational planning"; and a gradual shift of public spending away from programs that are redistributive in their objectives towards "social investment" spending, which supports those already at the "cutting edge" in their quest for being "world class." The drug scandals of 1988–89 point to the dangers of not working through all the assumptions underlying what is meant by these terms. It is our contention that these are effects whose desirability should, at least, be debated. We engage this debate as it relates to high-performance sport in chapter 10.

CHAPTER SIX

Gender and High-Performance Sport

I INTRODUCTION

One of the noteworthy aspects of our study was that equality of opportunity for females was a non-issue for most of the people who were responsible for the conduct of business and for taking the key decisions in these organizations. This flies in the face of recent efforts by the Women's Program of the Fitness and Amateur Sport Branch to redress the underrepresentation of females in both technical and decision-making positions in national sport organizations (NSOs). The most recent data gathered by the government show that women make up only 7 per cent of the ranks of Canada's national head coaches, 17 per cent of the technical directors, 24 per cent of the executive directors, and 21 per cent of the membership of the boards of directors of these organizations (Fitness and Amateur Sport 1985). These statistics, which are presented in table 1 along with other relevant data, have changed little since the first such study was carried out in 1980–81 (Fitness and Amateur Sport 1982): this in spite of mounting efforts by the Fitness and Amateur Sport Branch to improve the lot of women in sport.

These recent initiatives may be traced back to the establishment in 1967 of a Royal Commission on the Status of Women in Canada. One of the commission's findings, to the surprise of few, was that boys participated more often than girls in sports in Canadian schools. The report tabled by the commission included guidelines for future action by the government and women's organizations, but no immediate measures appear to have been taken by the federal government on the matter of equality in sport for women. Eventually, in anticipation of the commencement of the Decade of Women (1975–85), the federal government gave

Table 1
Female Participation Rates in NSOs by Job Category

	All NSOs			Six NSOs
Job Category	F&AS (1982)	F&AS (1985)	Macintosh et al. (1987a)	Macintosh et al. (1987a)
	%	%	%	%
Executive director	16	24	26	0
Technical director	18	17	22	12
Program coordinator	40	62	47	—
Head coach	14	7	—	0
Board of directors	18	21	—	19*

*Only 4 per cent on executive committees

financial support to hold a *National Conference on Women in Sport* in Toronto in 1974. A series of recommendations to enhance the participation of women came out of this conference. But despite these, and despite two national surveys that documented the underrepresentation of women in sport and physical activity in Canada (the 1972 Leisure Survey and the 1976 Fitness and Sport Survey), this issue was pushed to the background in the Canadian government's rush in the 1970s to promote high-performance sport. Neither the 1977 green nor the 1979 white paper by Iona Campagnolo (then minister of state for fitness and amateur sport) designated women as a target group for special attention.

A second national conference on women in sport and recreation was held in Vancouver in 1980, sponsored jointly by the federal government and the Institute for Human Performance at Simon Fraser University. The recommendations arising out of this conference finally bore fruit. It was one of the contributing factors in the establishment of the Canadian Association for the Advancement of Women and Sport (CAAWS) in the fall of that year. Since that time, CAAWS has become an important advocacy group for women in sport in Canada. Later that same year, the federal government established a Women's Program within the Fitness and Amateur Sport Branch. One of the first steps that was taken by this new division was the National Survey on Women in Sport Leadership (Fitness and Amateur Sport 1982). This survey documented for the first time the underrepresentation of women in high-performance sport (some of the data from this survey appear in table 1). As a consequence of this survey, the two major components of the Women's Program, the national association contributions program and the internship program for women athletes, were established. The first of these programs provided funds to NSOs for projects that would encourage greater participation by women in all aspects of the organizations' activities. The internship program initially had as its objective the encouragement of international-calibre female athletes to prepare for a career in sport leadership. But in 1983–84, the internship program was expanded to provide a seven-month on-the-job training program for both retired women athletes and female graduates of physical education and recreation programs. The culmination of all these efforts was the federal government's official *Women in Sport: A Sport Canada Policy* (Fitness and Amateur Sport 1986a), in many respects a path-breaking document. However, although these various initiatives have been effective in assisting women to gain access to entry-level positions in the National Sport and Recreation Centre (NSRC), they have not yet borne fruit at the higher echelons of the sport bureaucracy.

II CASE-STUDY INTERVIEWS

Our study focused on six high-profile Olympic NSOs in which there was a significant female participation rate. We pointed out in appendix A that we sought to interview key actors involved in the recent decision-making process of these organizations. These actors included the top-level administrative staff, key board members, prominent current and former athletes, and the Sport Canada consultants who provided the link between Fitness and Amateur Sport and the respective organizations. The ratios of males to females in key positions in these six NSOs in 1986–87 are presented in column 4 in table 1; these figures show an even greater gender bias than the statistics for all of the NSOs. Males occupied all of the six chief executive officer positions, 88 per cent (seven out of eight) of the technical director/manager/supervisor jobs, all of the posts as head national coach, and 81 per cent of the make-up of the board of directors. In the powerful executive committees of these associations, males comprised 96 per cent.

In conducting our interviews, we wanted to probe the extent to which NSOs had put into effect Sport Canada policy regarding the equalization of opportunities for women. In addition, we were interested in whether there were discernible differences of outlook between volunteers and professional staff with respect to the implementation of policies aimed at improving access for women. Certainly, there were personnel in the Fitness and Amateur Sport Branch, especially but not only within the Women's Program, who were professionally and personally committed to increasing access for women and to redressing historical imbalances.

Equally certainly, Sport Canada officially required (through quadrennial planning) that each sport address its own situation and include affirmative action in its future plans for coaching and administration, as well as in its competitive programs. At the same time, experience shows that when the individuals directly responsible for producing and/or implementing such plans are unsympathetic to the objectives (or are not themselves familiar with many dimensions of the problem), the results are less than hoped for. We were interested, therefore, in the extent to which NSO staff actively promoted affirmative action policies and the extent to which the volunteer members of executives within the associations either supported or had problems with such initiatives. Briefly, there was remarkably little concern expressed about underrepresentation of females in the positions of authority. Almost none of the males saw this as a genuinely important issue, and many of the females, while advocating "fairness," distanced themselves from what they saw as a "feminist" agenda.

The two most common reasons advanced by the interviewees, when pressed about the apparent underrepresentation of females in their sport, were that women were not forthcoming to fill positions, and that those women who did seek office did not bring the required credentials to the central technical, administrative, or volunteer positions in the organiza-tion. In the first instance, it was widely held that women, who bear the major responsibilities for maintaining families, found it very difficult to combine these responsibilities with the time demands placed on anyone aspiring to central positions in NSOs. This was seen as being particularly relevant in the case of positions that required a substantial commitment of time away from home on weekends. This, of course, is a requirement of almost all the central positions in NSOs.

There was also a view expressed by some of the interviewees that many former female athletes, when considering taking up a central post in their sport organization, often rejected it out of hand because they were too familiar with the tremendous "away-from-home" time commitment needed in the sport milieu. There was even sometimes a suggestion that women were too wise to take up positions so demanding and so poten-tially destructive of relationships. Why men, on the other hand, are more willing to sacrifice their home life in pursuit of public achievement stands out as an important question that our interviewees had apparently not examined.

In one team sport, the organization had shown itself more prepared than many other sports to hire female interns. National team graduates had been hired as technical interns and had progressed into coaching positions in the universities; an administrative intern was subsequently hired for a full-time job in the national office. In officiating, at least as many women as men had taken qualifications, although it was suggested by some that their progress through the ranks was slower because they did not make themselves as available for officiating assignments or courses as did their male counterparts. In coaching, there were a great many women coaching at the age group level but very few at the elite levels.

One not uncommon response to this lack of female coaches at the elite level, on the part of the men who predominated in club management and, therefore, on provincial and national committees, was to say that more women had to be willing to put in the time, attending weekend clinics and seminars, taking on officiating assignments, and spending holiday periods as assistant coaches with national and development teams. At the same time, it was suggested that women needed to get themselves on committees, and do the committee work that would subsequently get them elected to executive and representative positions. From the perspective of one male official: "There aren't any barriers to women in this sport. They just have to be willing to put in the time and effort, and they have to organize themselves and learn to politic."

From the viewpoint of some women, however, this not atypical male response demonstrates, at the very least, a lack of understanding of the problems women face when they try to combine active coaching or volunteer roles with professional and family roles. As one senior volunteer put it, "They just don't appreciate how difficult it is because they never do it themselves." Certainly, the men we interviewed seldom demonstrated any sense of the different demands which family life in our society makes on men and women, or of the structuring of male-female relationships in such a way that many men's participation and progress in public organizations (of which volunteer sport organizations are only one example) had routinely presumed upon the willingness of a female partner to "mind the home front." Conversely, women who proposed to take on extra-familial commitments which involved regular absences from the family, especially over supper hours and on weekends, were more likely than men to face family opposition and criticism, to experience self-doubt, and very probably, to face hard choices in which something had to be relinquished.

Our interview data forced us to reappraise just how powerfully women's domestic roles impaired their capacity to pursue these public roles effectively. Time and again, it was suggested to us that the routines of high-performance sport, involving many weekends away at competitions or committee meetings, or both, required regular absences from family life, absences which typically caused more conflict (internal conflicts as well as conflicts with spouses and children) for women than for men. Certainly, there are many mothers – as there are fathers – who, in the course of involvement with their own children's sport activities, give generously of their time at the age group/local level as coaches, officials, and organizers. However, the mother (or father) who wishes to pursue any of these "careers" to the national level must give much evening and weekend time to them. In a society where women are still generally expected – by their husbands, their children, and even themselves – to have primary domestic responsibility, the evidence suggests that such absences remain much more problematic for women. There are, of course, exceptions (and it needs to be reiterated that this analysis cannot by itself account for the obstacles faced by single and/or childless women). However, we heard sufficient accounts of the tensions between "adequate" performances of a woman's family role and the pursuit of a career in high-performance sport (and especially in coaching) to suggest that there are real obstacles to such careers for women, and that these obstacles are constituted by the gender structures of our society.

Here we take cognizance of the work of Theberge (1987). In research conducted for a study of the careers of women coaches in Canada, Theberge interviewed persons who were working and coaching at various levels in the sport system. Many of these people perceived that women were reluctant to pursue coaching careers because of the peculiar demands of high-performance sport. Thus, in the main interview process with female coaches, Theberge paid particular attention to the dual-career theory. However, she found that very few of the interviewees had curtailed their coaching careers because of family obligations. The older female coaches maintained that their family support system had accommodated the demands of high-performance coaching. The younger women, many of whom had not yet faced the problems of a dual career, did not anticipate such obstacles. It should be noted, however, that Theberge was interviewing those who were, in fact, engaged in coaching careers, and that many other women may have been diverted from such a course of action by dual-career barriers.

The second reason advanced for the paucity of females in key decision-making positions, that of lack of credentials, was in part borne out in our questionnaire survey of professional staff. The data presented in appendix B were based on an analysis of six job categories in the national sport bureaucracy. For the purposes of our analysis in this chapter, we dropped the category of "national coach" because of the almost complete absence of females. Likewise, the category "marketing and promotion" was eliminated because of the relatively small number of respondents and because

Table 2
Matched Pairs by Gender and Job Category

	Females				Totals	
Males	Exec. dir	Tech. dir.	Sport cons.	Prog. coor.	N	%
Executive director	5	3	2	4	14	41.2
Technical director	4	3	1	4	12	35.3
Sport consultant	1	1	1	0	3	8.8
Program coordinator	0	1	0	4	5	14.7
Totals N	10	8	4	12	34	
%	29.4	23.5	11.8	35.3		100.0

To compare the job categories held by the fourteen females who were matched to the fourteen male executive directors in this paired sample, one reads *across* the first row of figures in table 2. Thus, it can be seen that five of the fourteen females matched respectively to the fourteen male executive directors also held the position of executive director, three were technical directors, two sport consultants, and the remaining four matched females were program coordinators.

it was still a poorly defined position in most NSOs. These reconstructed data illustrated that the formal educational qualifications of female sport administrators were virtually identical to those of males. About 85 per cent held university degrees of one type or another and about half of these also had attained a master's degree. But in two other key credentials, those of personal sport experience and especially coaching experience, women lagged behind men. In the case of sport experience, 25 per cent of the males reported national open level or higher sport experience as compared to only 19 per cent of the females. This difference was much greater for coaching experience. Here, 35 per cent of the males had coached at the national open level or higher compared to only 11 per cent of the females.

That elite level coaching was a critical credential for subsequent appointments as technical director or national coach was borne out in a matched-pair analysis that we carried out on our questionnaire survey data (see table 2). We were able to match thirty-four female to male respondents on age, education, and personal sport experience. However, we still found within this matched matrix that females more often held program coordinator positions (twelve of the thirty-four females as compared to only five of the thirty-four males) and less often held technical director positions (eight females compared to twelve males). When the coaching credentials of the technical directors in our survey were examined according to gender, this discrepancy was made very clear. Fifty-eight per cent of the male technical directors in the NSRC had national open level or higher coaching experience as compared to only 13 per cent of female technical directors.

It may be wise to interject here that there are age discrepancies that may also be contributing to the apparent inability of females to penetrate the upper echelons of the sport bureaucracy. Our questionnaire survey indicated that the average age of the males was almost thirty-eight years, some five years older than the females. At the highest level of the bureaucracy, this age discrepancy was much greater. Male executive directors were eleven years older than their female counterparts. Not surprisingly, there was a parallel discrepancy in years of full-time experience in sport administration. The average of such experience for males was slightly more than six years; for females, this figure was 4.8 years. If length of experience is a significant factor in gaining access to high-level posts, then those concerned about the underrepresentation of females may have to be more patient about the rate at which women can reasonably be expected to gain better representation at the top levels of the sport organizations.

On the one hand, it is possible to see discrepancies in important kinds of experience as entirely justifying any gender inequalities that correspond. Indeed, the majority of respondents we interviewed held this view. Several explicitly argued that for senior technical positions in particular, national and international coaching experience was not only an advantage but a prerequisite. If this today favoured male candidates, so be it. At the same time, though, the interview data clearly suggested that women had difficulties in gaining access to the kind of coaching experiences which could "qualify" them by these criteria. In two sports, for example, it was noted that there was a long history of men coaching females and no history of women coaching adult males. This had made it difficult for women to break into coaching, even in club jobs.

This same history had also created an absence of role models for women who might aspire to high-performance coaching. It was suggested that while there were a considerable number of women coaching very successfully as volunteers at the age group level, the typical progression within a club program was that, as young competitors developed, they were passed on to the head coach, who was almost always male. Thus, until more of the strong Canadian clubs are willing to have women coaches working with their own elite prospects, women will have a hard time showing that they can produce the performers who would demonstrate their own coaching potential. Given the importance, moreover, of advanced coaching experience for subsequent access to technical directors positions, the frustration felt by women who had ambitions in these areas was well founded.

In another sport, there were some younger women, mostly former elite players, who were establishing successful coaching records in the universities and would thereby seem promising prospects for national-level appointments. The incumbent coach and assistant coach to the national women's team were men, however, and it might be suggested that, to the extent that experience was treated as a decisive factor in assessing the relative claims of otherwise qualified candidates, this operated against the progress of eminently able young women in coaching and officiating alike.

It was indeed true that male candidates for national officiating assignments as well as coaching positions could typically offer more experience. It may be legitimate, however, to ask how much experience is enough. It could even be argued that the weight which many sports appeared to give to experience, in a historical period in which demonstrably able female candidates tended to be younger, clearly favoured a different kind of leader than would be the case if there were a greater readiness to consider young candidates who had proven themselves in other ways. For the latter to become common practice, however, would clearly require a conviction that there was something positive to be gained by hiring young women.

This notion of the desirability of hiring young female coaches produced one of the clearest divisions of opinion between male and female respondents. Both insisted on the importance of technical knowledge. However, many of our female respondents, especially but not only in the team sports, argued that some male coaches apparently made little effort to understand the particular problems female athletes faced as women, and that a female coach could improve morale. Two respondents (from two different team sports) went so far as to suggest that morale problems on the women's squads were unlikely to be overcome until a woman was appointed as coach. Male respondents in these and other sports did not accept that this was an issue. They typically reemphasized the issue of experience, and one argued that "history shows that men coach women perfectly well." In the two sports where female respondents had alluded to problems, the male coaches were praised by other men in such words as "a real fighter for the women," "the best thing that ever happened to the women," and "by far the most qualified and experienced coach around."

Indeed, the role of qualifications and experience takes yet another twist when considering the gender balance of volunteer boards of directors, and especially the smaller management or executive committees, where important decisions were increasingly being made. In an organizational context in which NSOs were being required by Sport Canada to attend systematically to financial management and control, and in a political environment in which they were being pressed to raise increasing portions of their budgets from private sector sources, it was financial and fund-raising experience rather than sport experience that were coming to be seen as the most important qualifications for volunteers who occupied senior positions on boards. This view was made most explicit by one staff member who maintained that "The most important function of board members is now to open corporate doors."

It can be acknowledged that there was and is a real need for financial management and fund-raising skills on the boards of many NSOs. However, the suggestion that there was a hierarchy developing on some boards, in which "your influence on the board is related to your stature in the business community," pointed to yet another access barrier to females. This took on added significance, moreover, at a time when some NSOs were being encouraged by Sport Canada to restructure their boards to include more members-at-large in place of members elected to represent regional or other constituencies within the sport. These trends combined to favour candidates with corporate credentials; given the structure of the upper echelons of the Canadian work force, this usually meant men.

A corollary to "corporate credentials" was the suggestion that issues at the board level were often decided by aggressive debating tactics rather than on the strength of the arguments brought to the debate. These forceful debators were, not surprisingly, described as "men who are used to getting their own way in business." These habits of self-assertion, deriving arguably from practice in the art of confrontation, were seen by some of the women we interviewed as allowing males to control debate, and, in some instances, to trivialize gender issues in general as well as specific examples of gender discrimination that were brought to the attention of the board. An incident was described to us, for example, in which a proposed Committee on Women in Sport was referred to by a male executive as the COWS committee; this proposal died amidst raucous laughter. One male volunteer (in another sport) did wonder "whether we have simply shouted women down in the past, rather than prevailing because we had better arguments." However, such second thoughts were rare.

III   EXPLAINING BARRIERS TO CHANGE: THEORETICAL APPROACHES

In this section, we review three theoretical approaches to the problem of changing gender patterns, theories that focus attention at the level of the individual, the organization, and society, respectively. In the first two instances in particular, we draw on the work of Hall et al. (1989), who have contrasted representative analyses of the barriers that have confronted women aspiring to management positions in the business world, and sought to apply these lessons to the slow pace of change in Canadian sport organizations.

Work with an individualistic focus typically analyses the struggles of, and the pressures on, women who succeed in management (cf. Hennig and Jardim 1977; Morrison et al. 1987). Hennig and Jardim, for example, draw on interviews with a variety of older women who had achieved influential positions in the business world in the United States to formulate a more general analysis of what women must do in order to succeed in business organizations. The onus, Hennig and Jardim suggest, is on the individual woman, not only to qualify herself in the business and technical areas that are the subject matter of commerce and industry, but also to master the habits of thought and interpersonal behaviour that together establish the "authority" that is characteristic of successful managers, whether male or female. This emphasis on what the individual needs to do represents, in a more fully theorized form, the common sense understanding of the gender issue held by many men (and indeed, some women) within Canadian NSOs.

Certainly, there are examples in Canadian sport of talented and determined women succeeding. Abby Hoffman, director-general of Sport Canada, is the most well known of these women; but there are others who have achieved senior positions in the Sport Canada hierarchy. In the NSRC itself, women have started to achieve senior positions (i.e., executive director, high-performance director, technical director) in some of the smaller NSOs, as well as in NSOs where the women's version of the sport is technically different (e.g., gymnastics). However, as indicated earlier in this chapter, the evidence suggests that in the larger, high-profile sports, the senior professionals and, indeed, the senior volunteer board members remain overwhelmingly male. This is true, moreover, even though there is also evidence that young women are increasingly presenting at least the formal credentials (i.e., undergraduate and graduate degrees in physical education, sport sciences, sport administration, and commerce) that the system is demanding.

Indeed, it is their very emphasis on individual qualifications, and especially experience, that most clearly highlights the understanding of the
gender issue held by many men who today hold senior, "gatekeeper,"
positions in Canadian NSOs. These men regularly argued, as we pointed
out earlier in this chapter, that suitably qualified women were not available. They maintained that their organizations were prepared to hire
women, "other things being equal," and that women had only to put in
the weekend and evening work, and acquire the appropriate credentials
and experience. They pointed routinely to the exceptions (the same few
exceptions) as evidence of the system's openness. They even sometimes
pointed to the Women's Program and to Sport Canada's pressure on this
issue as evidence that women are favoured. Their view was that women
could make it if they really wanted to; therefore, there was no need for
institutional, let alone societal, change.

Ironically, the same insistence that the individual can transcend social
barriers also featured in the thinking of some (though not all) of the
women who have succeeded in Canadian sport. Indeed, the individualistic construction that these women put on their own success (a construction
very similar to that of Hennig and Jardim's subjects) may help to explain
their reluctance to push for more far-reaching organizational changes.
One respondent, for example, wanted no part of "women's lib," insisting
that "that stuff just distracts attention from the real issues." However, this
refusal to be identified with "women's issues" can also be read as indicative of the extent to which the task-oriented cultures of many organizations
ultimately shape many women who succeed (and survive) within them.
These women take on the attitudes and goals of their male counterparts
(cf. Hall et al. 1989). The managerial woman must learn to cope in a
man's world, even when this means becoming like a man. The problem
with this individual approach to rectifying gender imbalances, however,
is that it ignores the barriers that exist in the work-place, and indeed, in
society at large. It places the onus for change on individual women, and
ignores the difficulties that token women have historically experienced in
overwhelmingly male environments. Not only do these larger barriers
inhibit any marked changes in gender imbalances in the work-place, but
the resulting failures then become the responsibility of the individual
females in that work environment and they are left with feelings of inade-
quacy and failure (Kanter 1977).

This brings us to the second of the two theoretical approaches mentioned above, the organizational model, where the focus of attention is
on the structure of organizations and the work environment rather than
on the individuals in that environment. Here, Hall et al. (1989) draw

attention to a large and varied literature on organizational barriers to women's advancement, of which Rosabeth Kanter's work, *Men and Women of the Corporation* (1977), is an important and influential example (cf. commentaries by Hall et al. and by Knoppers 1987). As the title suggests, Kanter takes seriously the proposition that the collective behaviour of men in the corporate world has made things very difficult for even the most talented and determined women. Men's reluctance to accept leadership from women (exemplified in the male resistance to female coaches described above), men's stereotyping of women and refusal to take women seriously as colleagues, and men's collective refusal to take issues like child care and sexual harassment seriously have together added profoundly to the problems for women aspiring to management. These problems are especially acute, Kanter also notes, in those institutions where there is little history of women in leadership roles (the case in most Canadian NSOs), and where individuals who have succeeded are isolated and carry an additional burden of expectations (and self-expectations).

Kanter (1977) proposes that changing the gender balances of work organizations requires attention to three factors: opportunity, power, and proportion. Opportunity refers to "promotion rates from particular jobs" (ibid., 246); in other words, are women blocked at particular levels of the organizations (e.g., program coordinators)? Power refers to the "capacity to mobilize resources" (ibid., 247), both within the organization and on behalf of it. Proportion refers to the relative numbers of men and women within an organization, and especially at senior levels of the organization (ibid., 248). Kanter's argument here is that there is a critical proportion or breakthrough point, after which it becomes "normal" to have women at these levels. Women are there in sufficient numbers to support each other politically and emotionally, to act together to challenge sexist behaviours, and simply by their numbers to render such behaviours less legitimate and therefore less likely. Conversely, small proportions of women in the work-place make it inevitable that women come under pressure to conform to dominant male norms that exist in their work environment. It also makes it more likely that women will become discouraged about their career prospects and put less commitment into their careers, thereby fulfilling males' prophecies that they are "not willing to put in the time."

Kanter's solution to these problems is to emphasize organizational policies that promote changes within the institution that are designed to reduce the pressure on the "path-breaking" individual. She advocates "batch" hiring and promotion as one way to reduce the isolation and the pressure experienced by individual women. Although this has evidently been implemented in some large organizations in the United States, individual NSOs in Canada are simply too small for any block hiring of women in the higher echelons of any one organization. The women's internship programs referred to above, however, represent a more long-range approach to increasing the critical mass of women in the high-performance sport system as a whole.

Kanter also encourages women managers to "network," thereby providing the emotional support and practical advice for each other that is routinely available among men. This is another organizational change that Sport Canada has recognized as being important in its efforts to advance the cause of women in sport. Thus, Sport Canada supports "Au Feminin," the women's network that has been established in the NSRC. There is also support available, through Women's Program funding, for other less formal networking initiatives such as meetings of women coaches in a particular sport.

What is important about this literature is that it focuses on what organizations *can* do, as opposed to either blaming the victim (i.e., the individual-centred approach) or shrugging helplessly and pointing to society (or in this case, the family). Our interviews repeatedly confirm Hall et al.'s suggestion that, as far as most males in the sport system are concerned, women's family obligations are a societal given and, therefore, not something that NSOs can be expected to address. The organization-centred literature (cf., in particular, Ferguson 1984, as well as Kanter) challenges this refusal of responsibility. It calls on organizations that are serious about facilitating women's careers to respond constructively to this "reality": by providing accessible day care; by being more open to job sharing; and, especially, by restructuring job demands and job schedules so as to accommodate fuller participation by executives (both female and male) in family life.

Certainly, one of the most formidable organizational barriers that women face in all walks of life is the lack of adequate, affordable, and readily available day-care facilities. But because much of the work in NSOs takes place on the weekends and in the evenings, it is doubtful that even conventional day-care facilities would erase all the barriers that females currently face in sport. Sport organizations themselves need to take steps to set up their own child-care programs on the occasions of weekend and evening competitions, clinics, conferences, and board meetings. Such measures would not only enhance female participation in the affairs of the organizations, but would give a positive signal to aspiring young females who are considering combining a career in high-performance sport with the raising of a family.

Indeed, important themes here have been confirmed by Deem (1987), who has drawn attention to how much of male leisure (including, our data suggest, volunteer involvement as coaches, board members, etc.) is facilitated by women's servicing. Certainly, there was little recognition among the men we talked to that the time they had put into high-performance sport, the career experience they had thereby gained, and the seniority and influence they had thereby achieved had presumed upon a woman's domestic labour in ways that might have limited her own opportunities to grow. Deem argues that one of the most intractable constraints on women's leisure is precisely the continuing refusal of men, both individually and collectively, to take on the degree of domestic responsibility that would facilitate their spouses' pursuit of public careers.

At an institutional level, Deem sees these same males as affecting women's leisure opportunities in their roles as policy-makers and executives. Our interviews confirmed that few senior men in Canadian high-performance sport had seriously considered that the family dynamics described above, repeated across many families, continue to affect women's capacity to acquire the kinds of experience and qualifications now required of senior positions in the NSOs. Likewise, there was little sense among our male respondents of the importance of issues like child-care facilities in facilitating women's careers within NSOs. The tendency of men was to deny the need for such policies, or to say that it was "not sport's responsibility." At a time when most NSOs are under financial pressure and may be weighing the relative values of providing day-care facilities for female volunteers and, indeed, employees, against the expenditures in the ever-critical area of high-performance sport, it is our view that Sport Canada should take a leadership role by promoting and providing financial incentives to get such programs underway. It is encouraging to note that in the budget year 1987–88, provisions were made for NSOs to make submissions to the Women's Program for funds to support child-care costs at conferences and clinics that involve female conferees from out of town. On the other hand, efforts at the same time to establish day-care facilities in the new NSRC quarters in Ottawa were unsuccessful.

The work expectation in NSOs represents another powerful organizational barrier for females. It is literally impossible for those females who bear the responsibility for the majority of the home-care work also to meet the expectations involved in national-level sport positions. Betty Friedan (1988) sees the need for the restructuring of jobs at the management and professional level in our society as an essential next step (after the provision of universal day-care facilities) in order for women to make further advancements in upper-level occupations. Not only are the demands of such jobs inhibiting the further advancement of women, but many men are finding that they cannot sustain the expected work pace and maintain any kind of significant home life. We can offer only anecdotal evidence here, but one male executive indicated to us that his next weekend at home with his family was five months away, while in another sport it was suggested to us that almost all the national-level coaches were divorced. Thus, a restructuring of the work environment which would allow for a more reasonable work week would not only advance the cause of women but would also be of benefit to male administrators, and, in the long run, to the welfare of the NSOs themselves.

At the same time, there are obvious limits to which the time demands of coaching, and indeed of working with volunteer organizations, can be restructured. The job and school commitments of those one is working with mean that most of such work will always take place on evenings and weekends. More important, Hall et al. (1989) contend that even if job restructuring could be implemented (and they suggest that this remains highly problematic), it still fails to address the more subtle but no less fundamental processes through which male domination is sustained in organizations and through which masculine ways of doing things are routinely privileged in our society. At one level, the objection is that even when this strategy succeeds in winning access for women to sport and, indeed, in other institutions, the conditions of that access (for example, a willingness to work nights and weekends, and to put career ahead of family) effectively mean that institutional priorities and ways of working are not challenged by women's presence (cf. Birrell and Richter 1987; Theberge 1988).

At a deeper level, however, a theory that focuses on organizations and on change at the level of the organization cannot fully register the effects, on the organizational behaviours of men and women alike, of patterns of male-female relations that transcend these organizations, and indeed, the work-place itself. We refer here to the divisions of labour according to gender associated with family life in contemporary Canadian society, discussed above. We also refer, however, to the many practices that produce and reinforce male solidarity (including sporting practices, cf. Fine 1987; Whitson 1990), and more generally to the ideological practices that produce "standards" of masculinity and femininity. Kanter, we have already indicated, does point to the impact of some of these practices in the work-place. However, what we argue is that ultimately, analyses of gender in the work-place cannot be detached from analyses of gender in the family, from analyses of popular ideologies of femininity and masculinity, or from analyses of sexuality and indeed the politics of sexuality (see Hall et al. 1989, on "organizational sexuality"). Theories of the "middle range," such as theories of gender in organizations, in other words, need to be connected with more general theories about the significance of sex and gender relations in the overall structure of society (Connell 1987).

Two approaches predominate in attempts to theorize sex and gender relations at a societal level. The first, sex-role socialization, sees men and women socialized into masculine and feminine roles which are complementary and which are extensions of "natural" psychological and biological differences. The second perceives divisions of labour according to gender as the product of power relations. The "natural" expectations out of which roles are constituted are seen as being not natural at all, but rather the result of men's power over women, individually and collectively, in both private and public institutions. Hall (1989) points out that this latter approach to theorizing gender relations is in a relatively early stage of development and that different authors use different terms to describe men's collective relationship to women (e.g., "sexual politics," "the gender structure"). "What these formulations have in common, however, is that they define gender as a set of power relations whereby men, as a social group, have more power over women than women have over them" (ibid., 7). These relations are actively constructed, moreover, and have neither biological nor sociological necessity (cf. also Connell 1987; Smith 1987).

Sex-role socialization or role theory has its roots in an analysis of the structure and function of interdependent social institutions, in which the smooth reproduction of society requires the production of individuals able and willing to "fit in" to an efficient division of labour. Feminine and masculine roles correspond respectively to the demands of the nurturing tasks of the family and the different demands of the achievement-oriented public sphere. Thus, sex-role socialization is the necessary process of aligning the aspirations and skills of individual women and men with the needs of a gendered social system. In contrast, theories of sexual politics see social structures as constituted and reconstituted by power relations – patterns of relations between men and women – in which individual behaviour is modelled and is subjected to group pressures, but is not determined either by nature or by "system needs."

A systematic critique of the functionalism in which sex-role theory is rooted is not appropriate here (cf., for example, Connell 1987; Stacey and Thorne 1985). Briefly, the argument is that it is simply false to speak of structures or societies in the abstract as having needs. Only those groups whose activities continually constitute and reconstitute these structures have needs (Giddens 1982: 32), and the collective needs of men and women (like the needs of different classes and regional or ethnic groups) may well be in conflict.From this perspective, it is possible to argue that the very division of social roles into public and private ones, in which the latter are assigned to women while the former are materially rewarded and culturally valued, simply points to the historical power of men to define the situation to their own advantage.

In this respect, Rosenblum (1986) has pointed out how the construction of femininity and masculinity around the care/autonomy distinction has appropriated for the masculine those characteristics that are most positively valued in American society (cf. also Gilligan 1982; Hall 1987). This sets up a role conflict for female achievers, the social source of which is obscured by individualist rhetoric (based in psychology and in functionalist role theory), but which presents a problem for the "gender deviant" or "cross-sex typed" individual. Hall (1987) offers an incisive critique of the role conflict literature that even today distorts many discussions of women in sport by presenting the problem as a psychological one. In a similar vein, Birrell (1988) traces the development of the "women in sport" literature from one that was focused on individual factors and was sociologically innocent to an emerging "gender and sport" literature that is sensitive to the effects of many kinds of sporting practices in the maintenance of male power and privileges.

Indeed, Bryson (1987) underlines the contemporary role of sport, as an important element of popular culture, in the honouring of traditional versions of maleness. She proposes that the public associations of courage and strength with masculinity, which have been central to the social construction of sport (and beyond this to the social construction of gender), constitute one of the significant ways in which sport contributes to the maintenance of male power and privilege (cf. also Kidd 1987). She also argues that male hegemony is reproduced in three distinct but related areas of sporting practice: practices associated with the pursuit of domination (including verbal as well as physical domination); practices which reflect and reinforce men's economic control; and socio-political practices which perpetuate male control of the organizational machinery of sport (the practices that have largely been our focus here). The naturalness and the apparent necessity of all these practices are reinforced, moreover, when women apparently have to adapt *themselves* to them in order to progress, and when sporting institutions are not changed very significantly by women's entry into them. The dilemma, Bryson suggests, is that to compete on this terrain "almost of itself seems to promote dominant male values, ... Yet not to compete tends to confirm the stereotype of women as lacking" in the very forcefulness that such confrontations are intended to test (Bryson 1987: 358–9).

What these diverse, yet mutually reinforcing, practices point to is the existence of deeper patterns in male-female relations, patterns that necessarily form the background of policy debates, as well as the context of the practices we have described in NSOs and the attitudes expressed by individuals. We argue here that to think of these patterns as reflecting a *structure* of gender domination is to emphasize that phenomena as apparently diverse as divisions of labour in the family, patterns of leisure entitlement and the resulting access to certain kinds of important experience and qualifications, and the continued legitimacy of settling debates by verbal "force" are all parts of a whole – a structure of practices that work to the advantage of men and the disadvantage of women (cf. Connell 1987).

In sport, these different practices include the family practices and organizational practices described above. They also include a series of practices surrounding sexuality and the body: practices of self-presentation; patterns of physical empowerment (including, crucially, sport), whereby boys are more likely to be encouraged to learn to use their bodies in forceful and pre-emptive ways (cf. Connell 1983: chap. 2; MacKinnon 1987); and patterns of male aggression (verbal as well as physical) that constitute latent but ever-present threats for women (Deem 1987). Finally, they include ideological practices like the public/private division itself (cf. Imray and Middleton 1983), the use of androcentric language, homophobia, and many other ideological practices that organize the formation of individual identity around particular ways of being male and female. With regard to homophobia, we should note that in our interviews in the six NSOs, we encountered a number of male respondents who made remarks that equated feminism with lesbianism, and moreover considered this to be grounds for not considering individuals for coaching positions (Hall et al. 1989 connect this with their discussion of organizational sexuality).

It is important to note that this structure is larger than any of the specific institutions and practices that make it up. This is why understanding the *connections* between different institutional practices is so critical, and why strategies for achieving change within work organizations must address issues both as concrete as child care and as intangible as the ways in which men have either intimidated or trivialized women on committees. To theorize these different practices as constituting a *power* structure, moreover, is precisely to bring into focus the connections between the many different kinds of practices through which hegemonic masculinity reconstitutes itself.

IV   CONCLUSIONS

It can be reiterated that each of the arguments commonly used to justify women's relative underrepresentation in senior technical, administrative, and volunteer positions in Canadian high-performance sport – namely, unequal qualifications and experience, and the pressure of family responsibilities – can be seen to have some empirical basis. Yet these phenomena, as our respondents frequently made clear, need themselves to be grounded in structures of gender relations that transcend the boundaries of sport. We have argued, however, that to reify these structures, whether by seeing them as natural or as functionally necessary to society, is to obscure the effects of male power in many different social institutions, public and private alike. Moreover, where role theory typically suggests that changes in gender relations have occurred primarily as the result of outside determinations, e.g., economic and technological developments in the work-place, our data suggest that changes are being achieved (and retarded) as a result of struggles around specifically gender-related issues and practices (cf. Connell 1987; Craib 1987). Changes in the structured practices of the leadership of Canadian high-performance sport require, therefore, a theory capable of registering the dynamics of contemporary sexual politics, one that makes connections between work-place and familial issues, between structural and individual change, and between ideology and practice.

The importance of these gender-related struggles in the Canadian sport system cannot, in our view, be overstated. Our work convinced us that, within many NSOs, there is considerable resistance on the part of men to the idea that there is any need for an organizational response to gender inequities. It was put to us in many different ways that the relative absence of women from the decision-making echelons of Canadian sport was due to deficiencies that it was up to individual women aspirants to make up. Alternately, this relative absence was due to structures of Canadian family life that it was impossible for sport organizations to do anything about. At the same time, Sport Canada is committed to doing something about gender equity, at the level of both the individual and the organization. The Women's Program internships are clearly about helping individuals to acquire the requisite kinds of credentials and experience. At the organizational level, although batch hiring is inappropriate, given the small size of Canadian NSOs, the objective of the Women's Program is clearly to address the issue of "proportion" in an incremental and cumulative way.

However, it is important at this juncture to suggest that each of these objectives could be substantially achieved, and the Canadian sport system thereby opened up to appropriate women, without any significant effect either on Canadian sport or on gender relations in Canadian society. What this points to is the importance of getting beyond the distributional issue – the proportions of women and men at various levels in the sport system – important as this is, and addressing the larger effects of an emphasis on high-performance sport in the overall structure of gender relations referred to above. It is at least arguable that equity-oriented strategies only achieve the accommodation of women within an institution whose dominant meanings and values and practices are central in reinforcing masculine hegemony in contemporary societies (Birrell 1988; Bryson 1987).

The larger "relational" question is whether the institutions of sport could be transformed so that these effects could be neutralized or reversed. But only one of our respondents, an individual who speculated on what feminist coaching might look like, had begun to formulate this as a serious question. The issues surrounding "feminist transformations of sport" are explored in some detail by Birrell and Richter (1987), however, and we consider that their discussion raises several issues worth highlighting here. Their respondents sought to analyse what they had experienced as alienating in the traditional male model of sport, and they identified the following:

(1) the emphasis on the product – i.e., results, performance statistics, etc. – at the expense of the process – the experience of sport, the physical sensations, the self-education, the camaraderie and opportunities for emotional sharing;
(2) the tradition of hierarchical relationships in sport which apparently encourages managers and coaches to assume the right to behave in authoritarian and even abusive ways;
(3) the "elitism of skill", according to which the best players are honoured while the rest are ignored or belittled;
(4) the rationalized pursuit of performance goals or standards, at the expense of personal enjoyment and interpersonal support and friendships.

The last point in some ways restates the first, but Birrell and Richter connect their respondents' perceptions here with a point made by Gruneau (1983), Theberge (1985), and others that an emphasis on results "almost invariably leads to rational strategies for ensuring that end"

(Birrell and Richter 1987: 401). All of these phenomena are reinforced and, indeed, actively promoted in the model of sport being institutional- ized by Sport Canada. Our purpose here is to question whether a policy that promotes the meanings and values which surround high-perfor- mance sport is compatible with the broader project of restructuring gender relations in our society.

What this points to ultimately is that struggles to change or maintain the gender status quo in Canadian NSOs and debates over issues like day care, job reorganization, or consensus-seeking on committees are all connected: connected not only to each other, but beyond this to the larger struggle to challenge (or preserve) structures of relations between men and women which have historically empowered men and taken advantage of women. As Carrigan et al. (1985) observe, breaking with the notion of gender-specific roles (and with practices that construct such roles) is much more than a matter of breaking with conventional thinking. It threatens interconnected structures of power, changes in which would affect men and women everywhere. This is why struggles around gender relations arouse so much feeling. It is also why they are so important, and yet so difficult.

It should be added, finally, that it is important not to lapse into biological reductionism here, to imply that men in sport (or elsewhere) are inevitably aggressive, abusive, etc., while women are nurturing and gentle (Connell 1987; Craib 1987). The ultimate issue is not just the entry of women into a traditionally male institution, although this itself is important (Theberge 1985). On a deeper and more far-reaching level, what matters is whether this entry will be part of a transformation of sport – and, indeed, other task-oriented institutions – in ways that will undercut and challenge the hegemony of aggressive, rationalist ways of being in the entire culture (Birrell 1988; Markus 1987)

CHAPTER SEVEN

Equity vs High Performance

I INTRODUCTION

In the previous chapters, we have considered evidence that although the Canadian government is officially committed to gender equity and to the amelioration of regional inequalities within Canada, and although the rhetoric which surrounded Bill C-131 explicitly articulated the government's proposed initiatives in sport with the broader goal of increasing all Canadians' access to opportunities for cultural participation and development, the actual effects of the building of a Canadian sport system have been to subordinate issues of access and equity to the demands of high-performance sport. In this chapter, we review what appears to be a pattern in which official commitments to equity have been downplayed or lost in the business of establishing a performance-oriented sport system. We point to a number of specific areas of tension where commitments to equity come into regular and perhaps systematic conflict with the pursuit of high-performance sport. We refer briefly to findings that suggest that francophones are not well represented in the Canadian sport bureaucracy. The argument presented in chapter 5 that other kinds of regional inequality – between urban and rural Canada, and between wealthier provinces and poorer ones – may even be sharpened by the funding patterns that high-performance sport apparently demands is raised as well. We also discuss briefly findings that suggest that although Sport Canada remains committed to a democratization of Canadian sport, its Athlete Assistance Program (AAP) has not succeeded in altering significantly the socio-economic profile of Canadian athletes in Olympic sports. Findings that indicate that, within Canadian national sport organizations (NSOs), democratization and athletes' rights are largely treated as non-issues are also presented. The bulk of the analysis in this section, however, explores tensions between Sport Canada's efforts to promote gender equity in Canadian NSOs and messages that reinforce the dominant or "real" priorities of its high-performance system.

II   FRANCOPHONE INEQUITIES

In the early days of the professionalization of Canadian NSOs (i.e., the 1970s), leadership remained largely in the hands of volunteers. Studies by Beamish (1978), Hollands and Gruneau (1979), and Meisel and Lemieux (1972) in this era indicated that this leadership was drawn for the most part from middle-class Anglo-Saxon males, who dominated many other aspects of Canadian life. Francophones were conspicuously underrepresented. Our study investigated the demographic and socio-economic backgrounds of technical and administrative professionals working in the National Sport and Recreation Centre (NSRC) in June of 1986. Only 15 per cent of the respondents to our questionnaire gave French as their first language. For women, this figure was even lower; 93 per cent said that English was their first language. Only 50 per cent of the respondents stated that they were bilingual.

Studies of the composition of the ranks of Canada's high-performance athletes illustrate that the situation for francophones is little different. The most extensive research on this topic was carried out by Boileau et al. (1976); their study analysed francophone participation in all the major international games (Winter and Summer Olympics; Commonwealth; and Pan-American) for which records were available from 1908 until 1974. During this time period, the average francophone participation rate on Canadian teams in all these games was 8 per cent (ibid., 158). Post–World War II statistics were not significantly higher; only in the 1948 Summer and Winter Olympic competitions did francophone participation rates rise substantially above 10 per cent (the rate was 15 per cent for both the 1948 Winter and Summer Games). Gruneau's analysis (1976) of the composition of athletes at the Canada Winter Games in Saskatoon in 1971 confirmed the Boileau et al. data. Only in two sports did the francophone representation approach the proportion of francophones in the Canadian population (i.e., 27 per cent in the 1971 Canada census): weight lifting (31 per cent) and boxing (21 per cent). In the other sixteen sports in these Winter Games, the percentage of participating athletes from francophone backgrounds ranged from 2 to 17 per cent. Francophones made up only 12 per cent of the Canadian team at the 1984

Offe ⇒ 'lip service' ⇒ don't change conditions inequities
state + individual.   exist.

83   Equity vs High Performance

Summer Olympic Games in Los Angeles (personal communication with Bruce Kidd).

When the above figures are put into the perspective of the 1986 census statistics (Canada 1987: 2), which indicate that 24 per cent of the Canadian population had French as its first language, it is apparent not only that francophones are underrepresented in high-performance sport in this country but also that there have been few signs of improvement over the past decade or so. This lack of improvement was in spite of the fact that there was a series of francophone ministers of state for fitness and amateur sport during the Liberal federal government regime in the early 1980s. At least one of these ministers, Jacques Olivier, made efforts to redress this imbalance. Olivier took advantage of his official presence at the 1984 Winter Olympics in Sarajevo to make a public statement that NSOs, and indeed Sport Canada itself, had "stonewalled" bilingualism. He ordered Sport Canada officials to review all its own contracts to ensure that the principle of bilingualism was being upheld. Olivier also gave instructions to his public servants to hold back three-quarters of the monies that were being allocated to over one hundred sport federations until he had a chance to ensure that some level of bilingual services was being provided to their memberships. Twenty-two organizations were singled out for special attention (Macintosh et al. 1987b: 149–50).

Shortly after these pronouncements by Olivier, the Liberal government fell in the federal election of 1984 and Otto Jelinek became the new Conservative government minister of state for fitness and amateur sport. Jelinek did not bring to his office any discernible commitment to bilingualism. The uproar caused by Olivier soon died down, with little apparent effort on the part of NSOs or Sport Canada to redress this matter. But the issue still remains. Francophones are substantially underrepresented in the ranks of national sport administrators and, undoubtedly, on NSO executives.

Perhaps more serious is the charge laid by Olivier that Canada's high-performance sport structure has fallen well behind most other national organizations in the provision of bilingual services, particularly in coaching and technical services, and in translation at national meetings, coaching clinics, and seminars. Thus, any efforts to redress the current underrepresentation of francophones in the ranks of Canada's high-performance athletes will be hampered by the presence of this overwhelmingly anglophone national sport structure. If initial statements of intent are translated into practice, bilingualism in Canada's national sport structure is an issue that the second Conservative government minister with responsibilities for sport, Jean Charest, a francophone appointed in April of 1988, may pursue more vigorously.

III   REGIONAL INEQUITIES

With respect to the broader issues of regional inequality, our interviews suggest that the quest to rationalize the Canadian sport system is producing several dynamics whose effects are the opposite of redistributive. In chapter 5, we noted that centralization is leading to a further concentration of program resources in metropolitan regions that are already the best served in the country in this respect. Moreover, the increasing focus of NSO resources and energies on programs that directly or indirectly service national teams has meant a corresponding withdrawal from service provision to the grass roots. These services (especially clinics) were particularly important to clubs and schools in those less populous provinces that have not the means to provide such services systematically themselves. Sport Canada has recognized this; the 1988–92 quadrennial planning guide (Fitness and Amateur Sport 1988) includes a welcome directive on the importance of "domestic planning." However, as NSOs move towards "rational planning structures," which supplant the traditional politically representative decision-making structures, it becomes more difficult for representatives of those regions that stand to suffer most if NSOs withdraw from a domestic development role to mount any effective opposition.

IV   SOCIO-ECONOMIC INEQUITIES

Earlier studies of the composition of Canada's high-performance athletes (cf. Gruneau 1976; Kenyon 1977) showed that these levels of Canadian sport were dominated by male anglophones from middle and upper socio-economic class backgrounds. Much has been written on class and sport in Western industrialized nations. The interested reader is referred to Beamish (1978) and Gruneau (1976; 1983) for a sampling of these theoretical considerations. The pertinent question for our work, however, is whether governmental assistance through the AAP and, indirectly, through Sport Canada contributions towards high-performance facilities and programs in Olympic sports over the last decade has helped to enable Canadian men and women from poor economic circumstances to pursue high-performance sport careers. Clearly, one of the implicit goals of athlete assistance is to enable Canadian men and women from poorer economic circumstances to pursue excellence in the Olympic sports. In practice, however, it appears doubtful whether the assistance provided by the Canadian government, directly to individuals through the AAP and indirectly through Sport Canada contributions to facilities and programs oriented towards the elite, is enough to keep many poorer young men and women in high-performance sport.

There are examples of individuals in a few sports where high-calibre facilities and coaching are freely available in publicly supported institutions, and where personal equipment costs are minimal (e.g., track and basketball), and where, in addition, promising individuals are able to draw on other sources of support (e.g., a coach, or sponsorship arranged through a club). Here, AAP grants to athletes may mean the difference between getting by and not.

The problem, however, is that most promising athletes whose families are in poor economic circumstances do not have the financial wherewithal to reach the level of performance necessary to qualify for AAP support. That the personal cost to the athlete of training and competition associated with becoming an international athlete is high was confirmed in a recent study of Sport Canada's Athlete Assistance Program by Macintosh and Albinson (1985). This study pointed out that the "significant others" of Canada's national athletes (i.e., parents, spouses, friends, and sponsors) provided a substantial amount of the money needed for such training and competition (ibid., 20–1). The athletes in the Macintosh/Albinson study were being supported financially by the AAP. The financial barriers facing young aspiring athletes are exacerbated by the fact that they are not usually receiving the same level of financial support as are AAP athletes.

Two recent studies of Canada's high-performance athletes, one by Macintosh and Albinson (1985) and a second by Beamish and Johnson (1987), substantiate the hypothesis that recent governmental support to high-performance sport has not had any impact on the socio-economic mix of Canada's elite athletes. Both studies point to a substantial under-representation of people from low socio-economic status backgrounds in the ranks of Canada's AAP athletes. In fact, Beamish and Johnson concluded from the data they gathered from athletes supported by the AAP program in 1987 that the socio-economic composition of Canada's high-performance athletes was even less egalitarian than was the case when Gruneau (1976) undertook his study of the class composition of Canada Winter Games athletes in 1971. This, as Beamish and Johnson noted, is in spite of one of the avowed purposes of then federal minister John Munro's *Proposed Sports Policy for Canadians* (1970), that of eliminating inequities among socio-economic classes and of developing a broader, more democratic base of participation opportunities in sport.

This underrepresentation of athletes from lower socio-economic backgrounds is exacerbated further because most of the training sites for Canada's high-performance athletes are located in the country's universities. Macintosh and Albinson (1985) uncovered some startling statistics about the educational achievements of AAP athletes. One-quarter of the current AAP athletes had already obtained a university degree; another one-third had some university education. When the fact that about 10 per cent of these athletes were still of high-school age was taken into account, about two-thirds of these AAP athletes of university age had attended university. This extremely high university participation rate (when compared to figures for the Canadian population, which are estimated to be around 18 per cent) was confirmed by the figures for recently retired AAP athletes; over 50 per cent had obtained at least one university degree while another quarter had some university education. That the AAP program is very attractive to athletes who wish to combine higher education with high-performance training was also confirmed in the Macintosh/Albinson study. Athletes in the AAP program who were full-time students were more satisfied with the adequacy of government financial support, and with this level of support compared to their non-athlete peers, than were athletes who were either part-time students or non-students.

In fact, Macintosh and Albinson saw as one of the weaknesses of the AAP the fact that many athletes appeared to be using the program as a means of obtaining a university education and then dropping out of the program in order to devote their full energies to their professional careers once they had obtained their degrees. Thus, the AAP has become very attractive to athletes who have the economic and "cultural" capital to go to university. Not only do persons from working-class backgrounds stand much less chance of getting to university, but they are less comfortable in educational settings because of the predominantly middle-class values that prevail there. Thus, in many sports where the training grounds are first the secondary school and then the university, it is unreasonable to expect that an underrepresentation of people from working-class backgrounds in high-performance sport will be ameliorated until these conditions are changed.

V   DEMOCRATIZATION OF SPORT

A dimension of the democratization of the Canadian sport system involves the rights of high-performance athletes. The fact that athletes are partly dependent on AAP funding, and because of this on NSOs, has created some new tensions around athletes' rights. Athletes' opportunities to earn continued funding are at stake in selections for national teams (and, as well, for training camps and competitive tours). Athletes are also, in some instances, concerned about protection against arbitrary authority, especially surrounding training regimens and disciplinary issues. In this respect, although there remain some coaches and officials in some sports who still believe in a traditional authoritarian coach-athlete relationship, Sport Canada has actively promoted the use of published selection criteria and disciplinary codes, as well as written agreements between athletes and NSOs. Although these athlete agreements still vary among sports, they do mean that rights and obligations are spelled out in advance. Sport Canada has also pushed NSOs to establish procedures of due process.

Finally, Sport Canada has encouraged NSOs to involve athletes in the governance of their sports, with representation on committees and, in at least one instance, on the board of directors. Generally, however, compliance is at best unenthusiastic; NSO staffers as well as volunteer executives dwelt more often on the costs (in athletes' time and the sport's money) than on the benefits of such involvement. Indeed, in one sport, athletes who had been politically active were accused by a national coach of not being sufficiently "focused" on their training. In most sports, however, our interviews did not suggest a groundswell of athlete pressure for more active involvement in NSO affairs; it was suggested more than once that the most important athletes' rights issue remains poverty. For a much more exhaustive examination of athletes' rights in Canadian high-performance sport, the reader is referred to Beamish and Borowy (1988).

VI GENDER

The area in which the tensions between high-performance and social objectives are most available for analysis is that of gender equity, because it is in equalizing opportunities for women in Canadian sport that Sport Canada has made the most explicit and institutionalized commitment. During the 1984–88 quadrennial planning period, Sport Canada pressed NSOs to include planning for the development of female coaches and administrators in their high-performance planning. In the light of uneven progress, this policy became more explicit and pointed in the 1988–92 quadrennial planning document (Fitness and Amateur Sport 1988):

For the 1988–92 quadrennial and beyond, it is expected that the development of plans to meet the specific needs of women in sport will be a part of the ongoing Quadrennial Planning Process. Although there will not, therefore, be a need for specific women's planning committees per se, there may be a need to establish a task force on women in a particular sport to identify issues/concerns which could then be incorporated into the Quadrennial Planning Process.   (ibid., 4)

Through its Women's Program, moreover, Sport Canada has offered material incentives: both to individual women, to pursue technical and administrative careers in sport, and to NSOs, to encourage them to give women opportunities to do so. Specifically, the internship program has sought to address the standard reasons offered for the paucity of women in coaching and administration: namely, that few women have sought such posts, and that those who have done so have typically been less qualified than male candidates, who have offered superior combinations of credentials and appropriate high-level experience (see chap. 6). The internship program, therefore, encouraged young women with appropriate sport backgrounds to enter careers as sport professionals, while also preparing them to handle the prejudices they could expect to encounter. At the same time, it subsidized NSOs prepared to employ interns, and worked with them to design projects that would offer suitable kinds of work experience.

The internship program can point to some successes. Many interns have gone on to contract jobs in NSOs or elsewhere in Canadian sport. But only five of the forty-eight females who responded to our questionnaire survey had been enrolled in the internship program. Presumably, there were more graduates in term or contract positions in NSOs; we surveyed only persons listed in the NSRC directory. Moreover, although there was some increase in the percentage of women in coordinator (i.e., junior level) positions in the NSRC during the first half of the 1980s, there was little change in the percentage of women holding senior posts (see table 1 in chap. 6). In competitions for senior positions (e.g., executive and technical directors, or national coaching posts), especially in the high-profile and large-budget sports, women candidates are not being hired or even, for the most part, short-listed. What interests us here are not so much the reasons for this as the responses to it, in Sport Canada and in the NSOs themselves.

At one level, the Sport Canada response has been very constructive. The internship program has been substantially revamped; it now better addresses the current reality in which many young women in junior positions in NSOs (and in coaching positions below the national level) find their advancement blocked by male candidates with more senior kinds of experience. The program has now become essentially a career development program. Its objectives are to help selected women prepare themselves for leadership roles, through professional development experiences that are carefully designed to prepare the candidate for particular roles, and sometimes even for particular posts. The aim – in contrast with affirmative action programs that work on quotas, or that favour candidates from historically disadvantaged groups when qualifications are roughly equal – is to prepare particular women so that they *will* be the best candidates. This program is complemented, moreover, by other Women's Program initiatives that have supported clinics and workshops for women coaches, and encouraged networking among women involved in various roles in national and provincial sport organizations.

Despite these positive steps, however, two qualifications need to be registered. First, the resources available to the Women's Program to carry out its admirable initiatives are minuscule compared to the total dollars made available for sport by the federal government. In 1985–86, the Women's Program budget amounted to some $400,000. This represented less than 1 per cent of the total Fitness and Sport Canada contributions budgets (totalling some $58 million) in that year (Fitness and Amateur Sport 1986b). This budget not only limits how much professional development (and how many clinics and meetings) the Women's Program can sponsor, but also sends a message, which is quickly picked up by those who wish to read it in this way, about the relative priority of gender equity (and other kinds of equity) in Sport Canada's overall priorities.

In order to effect change within the present structure, it is apparent that funds in the NSOs' budgets will have to be redirected towards improving the lot of females. If Sport Canada is to be seen to be serious about changing the present gender status quo, it will need to bring more pressure to bear on the NSOs to use more of their budgets to this end. Until there is a real commitment by the NSOs themselves, change in the present gender imbalance in technical positions in the national sport structure will be slow at best. Certainly this is a problem that needs the attention of provincial sport ministries as well. Coaching apprenticeships and business management training programs at the provincial level are an important first step at this level.

It is encouraging to note that the Ontario government came forth in 1988 with a provincial policy for women in physical activity and sport (Ontario 1988). This document takes cognizance of the failures of previous efforts to provide equal opportunities for women in sport and makes strong statements about measures that the provincial government intends to take to rectify these inequities. Whether this resolve on the part of the Ontario government will be effective in overcoming the traditional inertia and resistance to change in gender participation on the part of most provincial and local sport organizations and leagues remains to be seen.

The second qualification we make about the impact of the Women's Program is that most of the board members and national office staff that we interviewed saw the "development of the sport" as the prime focus of their energy. Typically, they claimed that their sport had been open to female participants, and was quite prepared to devote extra resources to participation programs for girls and women that promised to contribute to the sport's overall high-performance objectives. There was also, in most (though not all) sports, some sensitivity to the absence of women from the senior echelons of coaching and in the national office. Some sports said they were prepared, as a result, to hire women over men, if qualifications were equal; most had been prepared to take advantage of internships and other special program funding from Sport Canada, wherever such extra funds were available.

At the same time, there was widespread resistance to being asked to implement affirmative action policies without special funding, especially where these policies did not directly contribute to high-performance objectives. This came through in resistance to the notion of hiring female administrators and (especially) coaches who were objectively less quali- fied than male applicants. The absence of female coaches had been discussed in several NSOs; typically, they maintained the position that technical excellence takes precedence over equity-related considerations. Resistance also came through more generally in comments that indicated that when there was great pressure on the resources of the office, and on the time and energies of its staff, people who were broadly sympathetic with women's issues still had to put their first energies into the high- performance-oriented tasks on which their own performance would be assessed. Indeed, one former intern, herself sympathetic to the objectives of equity, observed that, in the realities of her current job, women's programming came fifth, after development programming, quadrennial plan organization, financial control work, and fund raising.

One could object that such a formulation separates tasks that need to be seen as integrated (i.e., programming for women is an integral component of development programming, and of quadrennial planning). However, it is precisely this linkage that is not often made; in any event, the mixed messages that structure the NSO workplace are clearly high- lighted. The result is that most people in NSOs (professional and volunteers alike) see "the development of the sport" as their major task, and unless women's programs can be articulated with this task, they will receive a low priority. This conflict is compounded, moreover, by Sport Canada's own ways of evaluating an organization's performance, and evaluating staff performance. As long as organizations and individuals perceive themselves to be evaluated (and funded) in relation to high-performance achievements, other objectives will continue to receive less emphasis and energy. This is a question for Sport Canada to consider, for it is difficult to envision any other resolution at the level of individual NSOs. In the next chapter, we consider why this has happened and suggest some alternative explanations.

CHAPTER EIGHT

Social Policy and the Welfare State

I INTRODUCTION

In this chapter, we consider various arguments that have been used to justify increasing state involvement in the promotion of sport. Here, we compare the British experience to the Canadian. This leads, in turn, to a discussion of the historical debates about the proper role of the state in societies that value "freedom." We then discuss briefly the gradual extension of the welfare state to encompass many very different kinds of state intervention. Finally, we turn back to the question of the purposes and role of state intervention in sport in Canada.

We argue, drawing on work on the contemporary contradictions of the welfare state, that there are structural pressures that have moved many governments to redirect welfare or equity-oriented expenditures into programs that articulate more easily with the public relations goals of government and the corporate sector, as well as with the ideological premises of a market society and material pressures to expand the sphere of commodity production. This analysis suggests that those working in national sport organizations (NSOs) or in Sport Canada have little choice but to develop the most effective high-performance system they can, and that the equity-oriented programs the Women's Program *has* succeeded in instituting need to be recognized as imaginative and even brave initiatives, within a system whose structural pressures must remain performance-oriented.

In the next chapter, we consider a rather different analysis that addresses the role that changes in "sports discourse," have played in constructing what the new sports professionals, and indeed the politicians and the public, think are the purposes of sport. In this analysis, the political and economic pressures that are the focus of this chapter are by no means absent; but they are not seen as constituting, in themselves, an explanation of the decisive shift towards high-performance sport that we have documented in the previous chapters. Sport scientists and administrators are credited with a powerful collective role; thus, the specific character of the Canadian sport system is not seen simply as a product of structural developments, but also as the creation of active agents who believe in the value of high- performance sport and believe their job is to produce results, even when this comes into conflict with equity considerations.

In assessing this argument, however, it is also necessary to consider whether these technical and administrative sport professionals are not themselves products of a new kind of physical education (in turn, not unrelated to economic developments and academic politics), in which the rationalized production of sport performance has supplanted the traditional emphasis on education through the physical. This is the subject of chapter 9. Together, these chapters afford an analysis of the general issues of social process raised in chapter 1 – namely, the relationships among structures, agents, and ideologies – in the construction of the Canadian sport system.

II   SPORT AND THE STATE: QUESTIONS OF PURPOSE

On a number of fronts, we have sought to show that a preoccupation with high-performance results has conflicted with the pursuit of equity-related objectives that are explicit social policy goals of the Canadian government. We have pointed out that rectifying gender inequalities in the Canadian sport system is certainly a stated goal of Sport Canada (cf. Fitness and Amateur Sport 1988). However, we also argued in the last chapter that conflicting messages about its importance relative to the "presupposed system goals" of the high-performance sport system continue to complicate the achievement of this goal. In the other areas cited, the subordination of social policy objectives to high-performance requirements is, if anything, even more complete. At least in the case of gender, the existence of an official Sport Canada policy and the presence of a Women's Program puts some pressure on NSOs. With respect to the promotion of bilingualism and of francophones within the Canadian sport community, pressure has been sporadic and has depended on a francophone minister. The commitments to bilingualism articulated in the latest Task Force report (Canada 1988) are a positive sign. However, the history of the Women's Program suggests that a concrete commitment of staff and financial resources will be necessary if these verbal commitments are to translate into real change.

Some will doubtless claim that the relative absence of francophone coaches and administrators reflects the fact that few come forward, or that those who do are not as well qualified as anglophones. As with the gender issue, Sport Canada will have to decide how it wishes to address this. Even if the response is constructive, it can also be expected that there will be those who will claim that resources directed to making available bilingual services constitute a burden on their budgets. And they will be right. Again, Sport Canada and, beyond it, the Canadian government will have to decide whether more resources will be made available, or if not, how these conflicts are to be resolved.

The fundamental question raised here, in effect, is what the purposes of state involvement in sport are. One simple, and in many sporting circles taken-for-granted, answer is "to produce winners." From this perspective, articulated forcefully by the coach cited in our discussion of regionalism, government *support* of sport is necessary if Canadian athletes are to compete on equal terms with athletes from the Eastern Bloc and those Western European nations (e.g., Finland, France) where state subsidy of sport is institutionalized. Government interference with sport, however, was generally not welcomed in the NSOs that we studied. Especially unwelcome were those policies that hamstring sport organizations by requiring them to demonstrate equity in hiring procedures, to attend to development in the regions, or to spend money on committee meetings (let alone translation!). The above interviewee was sufficiently frustrated with even the current level of such requirements that he doubted "whether Canadians are willing to pay the price" required for international success. The price he alluded to, moreover, was not primarily financial, but rather referred to what he considered our preoccupation with democracy and equity and due process.

In contrast, Jean Charest, while welcoming the commitment of his 1988 task force report (*Toward 2000: Building Canada's Sport System*) to international success, and while promising considerable federal funding towards the realization of specific goals, also insisted that "We will as well want to address some of the difficult dilemmas and social goals that government shares some responsibility for, including access to bilingual services, gender equity, the integrity and ethical conduct of sport and other social challenges" (Minister's Overview, Canada 1988: 15). This, it can be suggested, is a necessary reiteration of the fact that many other performance-oriented organizations, both within and outside the public sector, simply have to accept that their performance objectives must be pursued within a framework that recognizes the laws of the land. Indeed, Ontario's implementation of pay equity legislation, however controversial, points to the growing legitimacy of the principle of private-sector responsibility in this area.

It may be useful, in trying to answer the question raised here, to briefly examine the objectives of government intervention in sport in another Western nation. We will then proceed to consider some theoretical analyses that suggest that the tensions described above between equity and performance might be products of our political and economic system: in other words, that they are the outcome of conflicting requirements that today contour social policy in all modern welfare states.

Our comparative analysis focuses on the United Kingdom, because in many respects both our tradition that sport should be left to volunteer-based sport organizations and our traditional understanding of the role of government in civil life owe much to British influence. There is also available a growing body of thoughtful work that traces growth and change in the British Sports Council. This work raises some of the same questions we are addressing here. Coalter et al. (1986), in particular, have documented changes in the purpose and the *modus operandi* of the Sports Council in a way that affords useful comparisons and contrasts with the Canadian experience.

The first British institutions established to help make and mediate government policy with respect to sport were advisory and at least partly voluntary. The Central Council for Physical Recreation (from 1945) and the Advisory Sports Council (from 1965) were made up of leaders appointed from the physical education profession and from the voluntary sports organizations, "to advise government on matters relating to the development of amateur sport and physical recreation, to foster co-operation among statutory authorities and voluntary organisations and to establish priorities for expenditure" (ibid., 49). What is notable here, first of all, is the presumed connection between sport and recreation. Indeed, in the early years there was a relative absence of concern with Olympic sport, which was still considered the preserve of the volunteer governing bodies. Secondly, these bodies were never more than advisory or mediating bodies, representing the views of the organized voluntary sector to government, and vice versa. Finally, these bodies were creatures first of the Ministry of Education and subsequently of the Ministry of Housing and Local Government. This, in Coalter et al.'s view, was an indicator of the extent to which the very idea of policy for sport was conceived largely as a component of urban social policy.

The establishment of an executive arm to the Sports Council in 1971 marked several changes in the government's involvement in sport and in its relationships with voluntary organizations. In respect to the latter, what stands out are the similarities with the Canadian experience. More money was made available for sport governing bodies; but the government was concerned that this be wisely spent. Thus, Sports Council advisers "worked with" sport organizations, just as their Canadian counterparts did, to develop appropriate structures of financial and program planning. This "modernization" of the voluntary sector involved a considerable infusion of public funds, but voluntary organizations were now held accountable for the effective and efficient use of such funds. This marked a shift from a supportive government role to a much more interventionist and directive one.

It is also worth noting that the Sports Council actively supported decision making by experts, and required (as did Sport Canada) that sport governing bodies "professionalize" their operations. The significance of this, in Coalter et al.'s (1986) view, is that the development of career structures, in coaching and especially in sport administration, became increasingly dependent upon the state, and indeed, upon the state's commitment to an interventionist policy (ibid., 52–5). Again, we suggest that this has much in common with Canadian developments, a point to be developed more fully in the next chapter.

At the same time, it is also important to point to some contrasts with respect to support for elite sport, and to the range of interests and objectives that are manifest in British Sports Council policies. On the one hand, the monies allotted to sport governing bodies increased steadily over the period 1972–82; the competitive orientation of many of the new sport professionals meant that much of this money was channelled into support for national teams (ibid., 55). On the other hand, the proportion of Sports Council expenditures going to the elite sector, incorporating National Sport Centres as well as national sport organizations, was only 45 per cent in 1981 (ibid., 65). In pursuit of its "Sport for All" mandate, the Sport Council continued to fund national centres for outdoor activities in Wales and Scotland, to give direct grants to local authorities for the purpose of recreationally oriented facilities and programming, and to fund various special programs such as inner-city football schemes (outside the normal frameworks of organized sport) that had explicit social policy objectives.

Indeed, the urban troubles of the early 1980s produced pressure on the Sports Council to participate even more substantially in the government's response to inner-city and racial tensions. Coalter et al. (1986) describe this as a shift from "recreational welfare" – the existing policy that saw recreational provision as part of the welfare state extending as far as special provision and programming aimed at groups identified as non-participants in sport, such as young mothers or Asian women (cf. the Sports Council's strategy document "Sport in the Community ... The Next Ten Years" 1982) – to a policy of "recreation as welfare." This moved sport into the front line of the government's response to the frustrations of inner-city young people. Programs like Action Sport, drawing on outreach techniques borrowed from social work and community development, were mounted in attempts to "penetrate sections of the working class and ethnic communities which previous initiatives had failed to reach" (ibid., 64).

There is, indeed, some history of Canadian governments trying to promote recreation as one answer to the unemployment of the 1930s (cf. Schrodt 1984). However, such policies clearly take us a long way from the Canadian government's current emphasis on high-performance sport; indeed, "recreation as welfare" is open to criticism from quite different perspectives. Those whose primary concern is youth unemployment or the structural nature of racial deprivation attack the pretence that sport programs are anything more than cheap palliatives that fail to address the root causes of unemployment, racial division, or urban unrest (cf. Carrington and Leaman 1985; Hargreaves 1985). At the same time, those whose focus is the stature of British sport decry this diversion of energies and resources nominally earmarked for sport into programs that have little to do with institutionalized sport and nothing to do with the development of support systems for British international athletes. Indeed, in a context in which direct assistance is much less available to British athletes than it is to Canadians, some commentators speak admiringly of Canada's perceived progress (Gratton 1988), and advocate strategies for British sport that owe more than a little to the Sport Canada model (cf. Anthony 1980; Coe 1985).

What the British experience does make clear, however, is that the equation of sport policy with policies for elite internationally oriented sport, which is now apparently a given in Canadian policy making, is neither natural nor necessary, but rather something to be debated. The debate, moreover, is not just about sport and the role of government in sport; it is also about the relationship of sport policy to other social policy objectives. Beyond this, it is about the role of government in addressing inequalities, especially in the institutions of civil society.

Clearly, it is legitimate to question, as did one former chairman of the Sports Council, whether organizations primarily responsible for sport should be "responsible for solving or helping to solve the social problems of our society? Is this not the rightful role of government?" (Walter Winterbottom, cited in Coalter et al. 1986: 62). However, the minister of the day considered that if government was to be involved with sport, it followed that policies for sport were part of the government's response to social challenges that every statutory agency, including the Sports Council, must be committed to addressing. Indeed, he said, "If sport didn't have any role in developing social purpose and social philosophy, it would be irrelevant" (Denis Howell, cited in Coalter et al. 1986: 62). Howell, of course, was a Labour minister, and not just the government but British society has changed radically since. It can be suggested, however, that the changes signalled by the "politics of Thatcherism" (cf. Hall and Jacques 1983) are not confined to Britain, although they are manifest there in a particularly stark form. They are changes that have seriously challenged the post-war Western consensus about the role of the state in social life.

III   THE STATE AND CIVIL SOCIETY

Classical liberal political theory saw the role of the state in society as something to be strictly limited: to the maintenance of order and the safeguarding of individual rights. Property rights, indeed, were foremost in the discourse of theorists like Hobbes and Locke; but they also enunciated a broader definition of a free society as one in which individuals were free from official interference. The state, according to these writers and their modern successors (e.g., Hayek 1960; Nozick 1974), can have only a very circumscribed role in the provision of social infrastructure, because the taxation necessary to fund such infrastructure constitutes an infringement of the property rights of individuals. The market is seen as the best mechanism for the production and allocation of goods and services, and market provision should remain the norm. Public provision should be embarked upon only when absolutely necessary: for public goods (like roads) which everyone benefits from, yet which are politically and economically problematic as market operations; and for a safety net that ensures the essentials of life to those who cannot afford market provision.

Clearly, both what is a "public good" and what is to be considered essential to human life are elastic concepts, and each has been the subject of much debate (cf. Ignatieff 1986; Walzer 1983). However, three aspects of this "minimal" conception of the state (cf. Nozick 1974) can be noted. First, welfare provision is not intended to serve everyone; it is selective rather than universal. Moreover, even where this principle is sacrificed to political considerations, provision (e.g., of public housing or transport) is typically funded at levels that mean that private alternatives remain preferable, or at least that dependence upon the public sector is experienced by most people as limiting. This means, of course, that motivation to regain access to the private sector is sustained; indeed, it is argued that high-quality public provision undermines individual and familial responsibility. Freedom and responsibility are stressed in this discourse rather than equity or distributive justice.

Second, the scope of the safety net is restricted to basic needs, which are seldom understood to include things like cultural or recreational provision. Coalter et al. (1986) suggest that those adopting this "residual and reluctant" perspective on collective provision are only persuaded to encompass public expenditure on sport and recreation when this can be convincingly articulated with the achievement of some other public good: savings in health care costs, keeping youth off the streets, and so forth. Roberts (1978) articulates this general functionalist case for limited and selective public expenditure on leisure in the British context. In Canada, Harvey and Proulx (1988) have suggested that this kind of reasoning runs through official Canadian justifications for expenditure on fitness and recreation: from the 1940s, when the promotion of fitness was seen as cheaper and less contentious than health insurance, to the 1970s, when Marc Lalonde (1974) saw fitness promotion and lifestyle change as important dimensions of the continuing battle against health care costs.

Third, the principle of insulating economic institutions (firms) and the institutions of civil society (of which sports' governing bodies are only one instance) from politics, and especially from political interference, is stressed and honoured, rhetorically at least. Thus, state assistance to private-sector partners and to voluntary agencies is considered preferable to the government's taking over responsibility. Indeed, it can be suggested that traditional associations among "leisure," "autonomy," and "the private sphere" have helped constitute an ideology in which government intervention is particularly to be resisted with respect to leisure activities and institutions. This ideology's residual strength is manifest in the still widespread belief that politics should be kept out of sport.

There is, however, another important tradition in Western political thought that articulates a more far-reaching and positive conception of freedom than Hayek's negative definition of it as the absence of legal and official constraint (Berlin 1969). A free society, in this more positive vision, is a social and political system in which opportunities for self-development are available to all citizens: not just in principle, but in fact (Macpherson

1973; 1985). This "developmental individualism" embodied a recognition that the constraints of poverty and economic dependence limit freedom in ways that are different but no less far-reaching than legal restraints. It, therefore, enunciated an active role for government in the achievement of "distributive justice" (Rawls 1971). This was to be attained through the provision of facilities and programs that would open up new possibilities for self-development among classes of people whose life choices had historically been very circumscribed.

"Citizenship rights," in this second discourse, were not limited to the necessities of life. They were extended to libraries and recreation facilities, as well as to opportunities to pursue excellence in the arts or sport, i.e., to participate in the forms of self-development honoured by the society (Mishra 1977). Indeed, leisure, seen as the realm of freedom and choice, was sometimes identified as a major arena for the realization of citizenship rights. As such, cultural provision and "cultural animation" – the active stimulation of cultural participation among non-participating social groups – were seen as important tasks of government (cf. Simpson 1976; Touraine 1974).

Certainly, the century 1880–1980 saw a steady, if always contested, growth in the scope of the welfare state in Western social democracies. This second vision of freedom, a vision that *embodied* a concern for equity (i.e., rather than seeing freedom and equality as antagonistic concepts), became the consensus of serious contenders for government. Indeed, for a time, the principle of citizenship rights was seldom publicly contested. Debate focused instead on how far it should extend (e.g., to concert halls? all-weather running tracks?), and on whether governments or voluntary agencies were the more appropriate administrative bodies. In Britain, Coalter et al. (1986) observed that, by 1975, it was officially considered that, "in a society which enjoys substantial leisure time," the provision of a wide range of recreational opportunities was "part of the general fabric of the social services" (ibid., 28). Other Western European nations (eg. Holland, Sweden, West Germany) have extended this thinking further still to encompass substantial support, in terms of facilities at least, for excellence in sport. In such provisions, we have come a long way from the minimal state.

IV   CONTRADICTIONS OF THE
WELFARE STATE

As Giddens (1982) has contended in his critique of the idea of "natural rights," it was always naïve to consider that the extension of citizenship rights represented an inevitable historical process, let alone demonstrated the moral superiority of democracy (cf. also Mishra 1977). Giddens points out that historical extensions of the principle of "social rights" (i.e., universal rights to new forms of collective provision) have always been vigorously contested by the propertied classes, as, indeed, have extensions of political and legal rights. Typically, new social rights have only been won – and it should be reiterated that welfare state provision has been a consistent goal of working-class politics, and indeed, today, of feminist politics – when they could be either articulated with the interests of the business sector (framed as the general interest, cf. Roberts 1978) or attached to the efforts of aspirant professions to establish new forms of social administration (again, in the interests of "society"; see chap. 4). This is borne out in Coalter et al.'s analysis (1986) of "recreational welfare" in Britain, and, more pointedly, in Harvey and Proulx's analysis (1988) of the Quebec government's interventions in fitness and amateur sport over the 1960s and 1970s.

Two points can be developed from these observations. The first is that the promise of equity that is embodied in the discourse of citizenship rights is compromised when provision for these rights is institutionalized in professional bureaucracies that have other, sometimes contradictory, objectives. Second, there is clearly today a political and ideological counter-offensive, which is present to a greater or lesser degree in all of the capitalist democracies, that seeks to deny the discourse of citizenship rights and to curtail equity-oriented government expenditures (cf. Giddens 1982; Macpherson 1985). In populist language, this is heard in renewed emphases on individual and family responsibilities, and in calls for "less government." The more sophisticated demand is that government expenditure be restructured so that it is more directly supportive of the health of the private sector.

In any event, the effect of this counter-offence has been that the priorities of public-sector bureaucrats are now shaped less by pressures to reduce inequities and extend citizenship rights, and more by demands for accountability and, especially, marketability. This is true even in an area like the sport bureaucracy that is, against this current, expanding. The least of these effects, Coalter et al. suggest, is that public facilities and programs are managed more along market-oriented lines. Beyond this, however, Gruneau (1984) suggests that we can see a general shift in the pattern of Canadian government expenditures on sport (including some provinces as well as the federal government), a shift away from support for low-profile and community-oriented projects and towards elite sport programs that create higher-profile opportunities for private-sector participation.

Our attention is directed here to what Offe (1984) and others have described as the contradictions of the welfare state. These contradictions can be traced to the fact that in order to be able to respond to democratic pressures for more and better services (i.e., social rights), the state becomes more dependent upon economic growth. Hence, governments must also institute programs and policies that meet the perceived needs of the business sector. The combined result of these very different pressures is the interventionist, "maximal," state of the post-war capitalist democracies. Such states not only encompass the equity-oriented welfare state measures pointed to above, but also embrace a series of measures that provide direct and indirect supports to business: tax incentives and development grants; spending programs designed to upgrade human resources (e.g., funding of higher education and adult retraining systems) as well as material ones (e.g., transport facilities); subsidization of research and development; and marketing assistance for export-oriented industries (cf. Macpherson 1985: 64–5).

Some analysts (cf. O'Connor 1973; Panitch 1977) have sought to categorize welfare state expenditures as oriented primarily towards "social investment" or "social consumption." The former category subsumes any developmental assistance or investment in infrastructure whose effect is to facilitate private investment and create opportunities for capital accumulation. The latter category refers to policies whose primary effect is to provide assistance to the disadvantaged. Such assistance comes either in the form of various direct grants to individuals or families, or in the form of public facilities and services. In this latter case, such assistance makes possible collective consumption (of public transit, education, housing, recreation, etc.) for those sectors of the population who cannot afford market provision (cf. Castells 1977). It also often provides such services for others who can afford them (cf. Dunleavy 1980). It is frequently argued that even expenditures on social consumption ultimately serve the interests of business: by sustaining demand, either through public works expenditures or increasing the spending power of low income families; by relieving businesses of direct responsibility for the social costs of production (e.g., unemployment insurance and injury compensation programs); and by reducing social conflict. Such expenditures thereby sustain the stability of the capitalist system (cf. Panitch 1977).

Offe's position (1984) is that these categories, "social investment" and "social consumption" (and others, like a division between accumulation

and legitimation "functions"), are useful in any analysis that draws attention to the fact that welfare state policies can serve quite disparate interests
at once. However, Offe considers that, in practice, the lines between
accumulation and legitimation functions, and between social investment
and social consumption, cannot easily be drawn. What is meant here is
that many programs that have been established in response to pressure
from disadvantaged social groups, and that offer real opportunities to
members of these groups, have been established in forms that also serve
the interests of particular business or professional groups (cf. also Dunleavy 1980; Saunders 1984). This is demonstrated in the establishment
of our national park system (cf. Bella 1987) and our public system of
tertiary education (cf. Axelrod 1982). It is also demonstrable in our sport
system. What needs to be emphasized here is the shift in state support
towards forms of sport that offer significant opportunities to the corporate sector (cf., for instance, Gruneau 1989; Gruneau and Cantelon
1987).

For the above reasons, the welfare state is angrily attacked from the
left and right alike. It still, however, represents a peace formula in which
many different interests are uneasily reconciled. Thus, it is also necessary
to recognize that in every area of social policy, policies will be subject to
these contradictory pressures. As a result, the outcomes will reflect the
capacity of different groups both to see that their interests are represented
and to define the issues that are at stake.

V   SPORT AND THE STATE REVISITED

In light of the above analyses, we are now in a position to reconsider the
question posed earlier: namely, what are the purposes of state intervention in sport? In other words, can the tensions we observed between high-
performance and social policy objectives in Canadian sport be seen as
products of the contradictions of the Western welfare state? If so, is there
any prospect that the routine subordination of equity concerns to the
production of performance will be reversed?

Gratton (1988) and Taylor (1988) consider that the production of
Olympic champions is something in which the state must take a leadership
role, because international success in sport is a "public good." For these
English economists, this means that the benefits of international sporting
success are such that everyone in the country shares in them. Gratton
cites a report prepared for the Sports Council by a committee, chaired by
former Olympic champion Sebastian Coe, that advanced four reasons
why sporting successes should be considered public goods:

(1) Sporting success makes people proud to be British. Sporting failure or decline has the reverse effect; we blame each other or ourselves and we feel less committed to the national cause.

(2) The link with prestige abroad is important. – If our teams and individuals are successful, they help sell the country's image abroad; thus directly and indirectly, they can help to sell our products and services.

(3) The Olympic Games create heroes and heroines. They encourage and inspire youngsters – and indeed people of all ages – to participate in sport, to develop and enjoy themselves.

(4) Finally, it seems right to us that elite achievers in any field should be given the freedom and opportunity so far as possible to realize their potential.   (cited by Gratton 1988: 2–3)

These benefits can be summarized as nation-building, international prestige, increased motivation for public participation in sport, and support for the development of excellence. Both Gratton and Taylor suggest that these are "public goods" precisely because they are "non-excludable," i.e., no one who is British can be prevented from sharing in the benefits, whether they have helped pay for them or not. Putting aside for a moment the question of whether many people really experience the first two as benefits, this is the economist's classic "free rider" problem: consumers who benefit in any case can choose not to pay. Thus, government typically provides the good freely, and finances this provision through taxation (cf. Gratton 1988: 2; Taylor 1988: 12).

Similar themes are manifest in the policy statements that have surrounded the establishment and expansion of the "Canadian sport system" (cf. Harvey and Proulx 1988; Macintosh et al. 1987b). Jean Charest, minister of state for fitness and amateur sport, welcoming *Toward 2000* (Canada 1988), stated: "While sport unites us at home, our athletes help the modern Canada become better known in other countries. In their own way, Canadian athletes and teams serve as ambassadors to the world" (ibid., 7). Charest suggested that the government "invests" in the Canadian sport system for these reasons, as well as to encourage participation and support the pursuit of excellence. Finally, government invests in order, said Charest, to see that the sport community does not entirely forget about bilingualism, gender and regional inequities, etc., while it is pursuing these other goals (ibid., 16–17).

What is also noteworthy in Charest's introduction to *Toward 2000* is not only the explicit use of the language of social investment but also the manner in which the lines between investment objectives and social consumption (or equity-oriented) objectives become blurred. Participation in sport is linked as well to health promotion (Canada 1988: 17; cf. also Campagnolo 1979). Opportunities for the development of excellence, which we linked above with the discourse of citizenship rights, are articulated with selling Canada's image abroad and with "opportunities for Canadians in general to observe ... and to draw important meanings from their performances" (Canada 1988: 16–17; emphasis ours). Everyone benefits, it is suggested, from the creation of a high-performance sport system, just as Gratton and Taylor would have us believe. Opportunities for capital accumulation are created, and the system also creates developmental opportunities for ordinary Canadians, as well as improving public morale.

Noteworthy as well in *Toward 2000* is the reiteration of the government's central role in the achievement of these public goals: "Further, if broader social goals (eg. gender equality, enhanced regional access, Canadian prominence on the world stage, etc.) are to be accomplished *in* and *through* sport, a stronger governmental presence in leadership and financial terms is also required" (ibid., 29). On the one hand, there is a clear acknowledgment here that the provision of non-economic facilities and subsidies is only likely to be undertaken by government, and that the responsibilities of governments to pursue broader social goals reinforce the need for a strong government presence. What is questionable, in our view, is the supposition that "Canadian prominence on the world stage" is a social goal of the same order as gender equality or enhanced regional access to sporting opportunities.

We are returned here to the contradictions of the welfare state, and in particular to Macpherson's discussion (1985: 70–3) of the state's need to legitimate its activities, not just to popular opinion, but also to capital. In this respect, it is not only that "The lexicon of business, finance, and marketing is now well established in the working culture of many sports" (Canada 1988: 26); the project of marketing Olympic sport to private sector sponsors constitutes an effort to bring corporations "on side" by persuading them that promoting sport can be a part of their own marketing strategies.

In a very material sense, high-performance sport offers to large corporations certain other kinds of opportunities for investment and profit. It is quite clear that the media coverage now given to international sport competitions creates opportunities for national television exposure for large corporate sponsors. Even more concretely, the staging of international events (which is not unrelated to stature in the world of international sport) offers very lucrative opportunities for the construction and tourist industries, the communications industries, and other corporate sponsors

of elite sport. This is why the corporate sector has enthusiastically supported the efforts of Canadian cities to stage Olympic and Commonwealth
games.

In an ideological sense, moreover, it is arguable that the messages of
high-performance sport reinforce the legitimacy of a competitive society
in a way that recreational sport does not. Certainly, the meanings Canadians were encouraged to draw from the advertising that surrounded the
Seoul and Calgary Olympics emphasized the importance of individual
struggle and the support of family and coach, as well as the legitimacy of
a meritocracy. At the same time, it can be argued that the nationalist
rhetoric that is so much a part of government discourse about international
sport today (and not just in Canada, of course, but also in Britain, as we
have seen, and other Western nations, and in the socialist countries
and the developing world as well) is at least partly about strengthening
identification with national elites. In other words, the project of nation
building or social integration is assisted by popular symbols that serve to
construct "we-they" identifications along national lines (rather than class,
or ethnic, or regional lines; cf. Hall and Jacques 1983). International sport
has long offered a ready source of such symbols (cf. Goodhart and
Chataway 1968).

Together, these material and ideological factors lend support to Gruneau's contention (1984) that the historical shift we have observed in the
character of state support for sport – a shift away from forms of grant
support that enable local governments and voluntary agencies to fund
recreationally oriented sport programs at the grass-roots level, and
towards the direct involvement of national government in elite sport
programs – is at least consistent with the interests of capital. Certainly,
our interviews confirm that the pursuit of prominence on the world stage
has tended to push issues like gender equity and regional access into the
background, and that the discourse that today surrounds the Canadian
sport system is one in which broader social goals are routinely subordinated to the production of performance.

Macpherson and others (cf. Dunleavy 1980; Offe 1984), however,
suggest that phenomena like this (the subordination of broader social
goals) are seldom simply a matter of the needs of capital; rather, they
also reflect political and ideological campaigns that seek to define the
way that issues are addressed. If further illustration is needed of the
effects of such issue definition, it is demonstrated in *Toward 2000*. The
suggestion is made, apparently seriously, that within the next four years
Canadians "should see some progress with the basic question 'What
does it cost to be number one in the world in sport x ... ?' " (Canada

1988: 26). Putting aside for the moment that neutral observers might consider it presumptuous that Canada should expect to place "among the three leading Western sporting nations (with West Germany and the U.S.A.) – in the 1992 Summer Olympics" and "first as a nation in the 1990 Commonwealth Games" (ibid., 36), what is remarkable here is that this "basic question" is deemed worth asking, and is apparently one we are committed to answering. It is especially remarkable when, despite repeated references in the document to the importance of working to achieve bilingualism, gender equality, and regional access to sport (and the reference to these issues is to be commended), the idea that we might find out (and in a finite time period) what it might cost to achieve these equity goals is never seriously raised.

What is also clearly underlined is that the issue is not money; rather, it is one of priorities and political will. Indeed, Gruneau (1984) has observed that in the early 1980s in British Columbia, Premier Bennett increased expenditures on high-performance sport and provided substantial subsidies for the construction of BC Place at the same time that he insisted that his government could not afford social programs. As Goodale (1985) remarks: "No doubt there is an economic limit to the total amount of goods and services that can be produced. But within that limit, social and political values determine what is produced and who gets it. A budget, therefore, is an allocation based not on dollars but on values: it converts resources into human purposes" (ibid., 198). It is this question of purpose that the Canadian government must face in respect to its involvement in sport; the evidence suggests that it is obscured by talk about the "needs" of the Canadian sport system.

In this chapter, we have considered arguments that suggest that these trends in high-performance sport reflect growing pressures on the Canadian state to legitimate itself to capital, and to articulate all forms of social provision more closely with the requirements of capital accumulation. It is clear that we consider that such pressures exist. It should also be clear, however, that we consider that changes in the nature and objectives of social provision cannot be reduced to a description of "system needs," whether these refer to the needs of capitalism or the needs of sport. It is necessary, in both cases, to take seriously the political processes through which some interests are systematically represented while others are marginalized. It is also necessary to understand the ideological processes through which professional (and lay) understandings of "system needs" are constructed and shaped. It is especially to this latter task that we turn in the next chapter.

CHAPTER NINE

The Reconstruction of the Physical Education Profession

For every (isolatable) ... cultural area ... whose relations can be analysed in terms of presupposed system goals, a new discipline emerges in the social sciences.

(Habermas 1971: 56)

The professional is constituted as much by his or her ideological preparation as by technical education. (Aronowitz and Giroux 1985: 188)

I INTRODUCTION

The dramatic growth in the number of technical and administrative staff members in provincial and national sport organizations (NSOs) was documented in chapter 1. We also argued that, by most agreed criteria, this new breed of full-time sport administrators now constitutes at the very least a semi-profession or aspirant profession. Indeed, we see this emerging sport management profession as representing another generation of that same "branching" process within intellectual and professional specialisms (often themselves marginal) that produced physical education itself at the turn of the century (cf. Larson 1984 and Johnston and Robbins 1977 on "scientific branching"). The reader is specifically referred to Lawson's account (1985) of the "claims to jurisdiction" over selected "needs and problems" which surrounded the establishment of physical education, educational administration, educational psychology, etc., in the early part of this century, and to Slack's analyses (Slack 1985; Slack and Hinings 1987a) of bureaucratization and organizational change in Canadian NSOs. Slack and his colleagues are interested in the professionalization of provincial and national voluntary sport organizations from the perspective of organizational theory, and seek a more sophisticated understanding of how to manage organizational change (cf. Hinings and Slack 1987; Slack 1985; Slack and Hinings 1987a; Thibault et al. 1988). In this chapter, however, we wish to explore professionalization as a political and ideological accomplishment and seek to explicate the significance of the same developments from the perspective of political theory.

We acknowledge that the professionalization of these provincial and national sport bureaucracies can, from a functionalist standpoint, be seen simply as a rational and, indeed, necessary response to the environmental imperatives, to an increasingly competitive and sophisticated task environment (i.e., the world of international sport), and to their own dependence for funding upon governments that have tied funding levels to success in that environment. However, this analysis, although accurate as far as it goes, skates smoothly past the very questions that we found most interesting. In particular, it fails to credit the extent to which these changes have involved real power struggles, in which some interest groups and coalitions of interests have gained influence (including the sport management professionals themselves), while others have lost it.

More generally, functionalist theories seldom address in any critical way the ideological processes that are involved in the successful establishment of a profession's knowledge claims. We felt this to be of particular importance, for, as Lawson's discussions (1984; 1985) of the knowledge claims of physical educators make clear, the claim to professional status involves a claim to mastery of a specialized, theoretically based, and socially valuable body of knowledge. As Lawson observed (1985), this is seldom a straightforward task.

Rather it is achieved through social negotiations, involving contests with other aspirant and existing professions, as well as with would-be clients. These contests include debate over competing definitions of knowledge and human need. Ultimately, would-be clients must be convinced that the profession, by virtue of its expertise, offers services they need but cannot provide for themselves.   (ibid., 9)

These are exactly the sort of contests and debates that our interviews suggest have characterized the professionalization of Canadian sport. Some NSOs have been enthusiastic converts, while others have endured conflicts that have become very personalized. We consider that the underlying issue, however, is the claim that the sport sciences discipline and its quasi-professions, including "sport management," that are based upon it offer Canadian society services that it needs and that volunteer-directed sport organizations cannot provide. Often this issue is complicated, moreover, by the recognition that once issues are institutionally defined as requiring expert input, the capacity of lay citizens (i.e., volunteers) to challenge the experts' policies is seriously undercut (Offe 1984: 168). This theme was developed more fully in chapter 4.

As mentioned above, we are less interested here in how organizational change can be accomplished or managed than in clarifying how particular ideas and interest groups have triumphed, and with the political effects of these triumphs. Thus, in this chapter, we consider "sport sciences," and its dependent professions, including "sport management," as linguistic and socio-historical constructs representing the efforts of an aspirant profession to link its own special knowledge with "ideas in good standing" (Schon 1979), and with the projects of other important interest groups.

At the same time, because our interviews confirmed Geison's observation (1983) that professionals are usually completely sincere in their advocacy of the value of their disciplinary knowledge (cf. chap. 2), we want to understand how these new sport management professionals have themselves been shaped by the discourses they have learned in their undergraduate and graduate programs in the sport sciences and in sport administration. In this chapter, we argue that these new discourses (whatever terminology is used to name them) have had an important effect in constructing not only what the graduates of such programs "know," but also how they understand the nature of their expertise, and how they see their own mission and their professional role in Canadian high-performance sport.

II   LANGUAGE AND PROFESSIONALISM

In considering the role of language in "accomplishing profession" (Dingwall 1976), our starting point is Brown's contention (1986) that each new group of would-be professionals has both to define, organize, and publicize its own particular expertise as well as to define for the public the role it sees for itself in meeting the social needs it defines. This analysis connects with Foucault's point (1980) that we have difficulty thinking beyond the knowledge structures which "define the situation" and, indeed, define our "needs" for us in a host of different institutions: from the prison and the hospital to the gymnasium and the bedroom. Foucault's argument is that advocates of successive "disciplines," or sciences of human behaviour, define what is "normal" in successive areas of life, and then treat all departures from these norms as "deviant," and as proper objects of research, management, counselling, and therapy. In doing so, of course, they construct particular social (and political) roles for themselves as researchers, managers, and therapists.

It is in just this way that Harvey and Proulx (1988) suggest that many educated groups of middle-class quasi-professionals succeeded through the 1960s and 1970s in creating roles for themselves in the formation and implementation of social policy. More specifically, Harvey and Proulx argue that Quebec physical educators were able, through their representation on the Belisle Commission (a body set up by the provincial government in the early 1960s to study leisure, physical education, and sport in the province of Quebec) to develop a blueprint that included a central role for their profession in the future development of sport and recreation in the province. As a result, the Quebec government became convinced of the desirability, even the need, to employ university graduates of physical education and recreation programs to ensure that sport and recreation programs in Quebec would meet the "needs" (as perceived by these professionals) of the people of that province.

Another perspective on professional language is offered by Hudson (1978), who argues that specialist language plays a vital role in maintaining the boundaries between those who are part of the professional community and those who are not. The confident use of jargon, he suggests, reinforces the hierarchy of knowledge in which theoretical and conceptual knowledge, grounded in formal training, carries more weight than the practical or experiential knowledge of the coach or administrator, for example. Practitioners may be privately sceptical of the value of academic knowledge, but jargon renders it more difficult to challenge.

Brown (1986) points out, however, that alongside this "mystifying" function, professional language must also present the profession to society in such a way that its contribution is understood and desired. This latter task, she suggests, is especially important for aspirant professionals who must popularize their work, yet do so without rendering their knowledge so accessible that it is no longer marketable. This role construction is never easy or automatic, for, as Brown points out, "An inherent tension arises between the twin tasks of *popularizing* one's contribution to society, so that it is comprehensible enough to be appreciated, and *monopolizing* one's knowledge, so that it is incomprehensible enough to be marketable" (ibid., 37). Managing this tension is especially difficult in cases like recreation and sport, where the knowledge base concerns experiences that virtually everyone believes they know something about (cf. Wilensky 1964). However, Brown (1986) suggests that these conflicting tasks can be managed by aspiring professions more effectively by "linguistic modelling" – the use of metaphor and association to model their own professional enterprise upon the cultural authority of an established and respected one (ibid., 39; cf. also Schon 1979).

The essential insight here, of course, is simply that meaning resides not so much in individual words or images but in the ways they are put together, the associations that are established and the connotations traded on. This is something that, needless to say, has long been understood in advertising and in politics (cf. Edelman 1977). Likewise, Brown (1986) suggests, metaphor and association enable professionals to present themselves and their expertise to society in a way that avoids detailed debate about the real content or social value of their expertise. Indeed, Edelman (1977) depicts this very process at work in the presentation of "recreation therapy" as a professional activity: "Mental patients do not hold dances; they have dance therapy. If they play volleyball, that is recreation therapy" (ibid., 59–60). In the construct of "recreation therapy," what was once left to hospital aides and volunteers is now associated with what most people consider a purely professional role, that of the therapist, and beyond this with the notion of a body of task-specific expertise (as in physiotherapy or occupational therapy). Similar comments could be made about the construction and presentation of "sport management" as a professional activity.

Brown (1986) also suggests that in the early days of an aspirant profession's attempt to popularize its contribution, it often draws on several different metaphors. It does so because of real debate within the profession, as well as its need to create a clientele out of often quite disparate interest groups. Indeed, commentators on the professionalization of physical education in Canada (cf. Guay 1981; Zeigler 1983) and England (cf. Fletcher 1984; Mangan 1981) allude to the presence of many different discourses – of medicine and health, military preparedness, social work, and moral education – in the early efforts of physical education to sell itself to a public preoccupied by other matters. Each of these discourses sought in its own way to associate physical education with the goals of important constituencies. Brown goes on to argue, however, that the presence of competing metaphors sustains a creative tension within a profession about the nature of its distinctive expertise, a tension which is lost when professional discourse consolidates around a dominant metaphor. In these circumstances, professional language loses its metaphorical character. It becomes literal and it excludes not only lay persons but persons within the profession who raise heretical questions and insist on the validity of other languages.

As physical education is being reconstructed today as "sport sciences," professional discourse is consolidated around the languages of science and management, trading on the cultural authority of these two models of knowledge and of professional practice. In the case of the sport science "discipline," an explosion of semi-popular as well as academic literature (ranging, for example, from *The Science of Hurdling* to the *Canadian Journal of Sport Sciences*) seeks to construct a science of human performance on the model of the natural sciences, and to present scientific knowledge of sport as clearly superior to the practical and personal knowledge of an earlier generation of coaches.

Indeed, the development of the national coaching certification program during the 1970s, in which a number of sport scientists from Canadian universities participated extensively, is another example of how university physical educators and sport scientists were able to establish and "mystify" a new profession to the extent that only university-trained personnel are now seen as being capable of defining and providing instruction in the "science" of coaching. The emergence of the national coaching certification program provides perhaps the most pointed instance in the field of sport and physical education in Williams's account (1976) of shifts in the meanings attached to "expert." He describes how the term used to refer to one who stood out because of his/her experience and demonstrable success, but how now, at least for purposes of employment and official recognition, it has come to mean one who is distinguished by one's credentials. In this endeavour, the emergent sport sciences were following a path blazed by earlier generations of sociologists and psychologists seeking to establish the legitimacy of their own enterprise by associating it with the cultural authority of science. We are not saying here that there is no hard scientific content in biomechanics, exercise physiology, etc., although we agree with Beamish (1982) and Demers (1988) that sport research carried out within this framework is structured by certain biases and assumptions that set the agenda and establish the type of questions that will be asked.

In the case of sport management, another prestigious social metaphor is involved. Older discourses of "leadership" and even "administration" are being supplanted by one that articulates the language of bureaucratic rationalization with the buzzwords of an "entrepreneurial culture" (e.g., "results orientation," "marketing," "bottom line"). The significant thing about the discourse of management, in MacIntyre's view (1981), is that it diffuses the idioms and the assumptions of business into many institutions that are not, at least in their original purposes, businesses. MacIntyre contends (ibid., 71–5, 100–2) that the notion of "management science" is a cultural fiction and that management training primarily involves initiation into an ideology and an institutional role rather than into technical skills. Such a position is clearly polemical, but it points to something evidenced in management guru Peter Drucker's contention (1974) that what management actually involves is defined by "the specific ... mission of their institution" and by "making work productive and the worker achieving" (ibid., 40–2; cited by Hardy 1987: 208). What is arguably common to the discourses of sport science and sport management alike is that they construct the nature of the sport professional's pursuit of knowledge in highly specific and narrowly task-oriented ways.

Much of the research in sport sciences and sport management focuses on the search for the most effective techniques by which to achieve optimal output: in the former case from the "programmed body" of the athlete (Harvey 1983); in the latter, from the restructured and profession-ally managed sport organization (Slack and Hinings 1987a). In either case, a role is constructed for the sport professionals that, in its responsibil-ity for the "production of performance" (whether in the athletes or in the national sport organization), is distinctly different from that of the traditional physical educator. The physical educator was expected to be concerned with the development of the individual, and was often criticized if (s)he subordinated this to the pursuit of performance. Changes in the knowledge of structures of physical education, in other words, and in its dominant "problem-definitions," cannot be detached from struggles to redefine the profession's mission (Lawson 1984).

There were a number of factors that contributed to the move to a greater science emphasis in physical education degree programs in Canadian universities. In the first place, many of the physical educators who joined burgeoning departments and faculties of physical education in Canadian universities in the 1960s and early 1970s held post-graduate degrees from universities in the United States. Graduate physical education and research programs in these American institutions had, as, indeed, had all American education, been very much influenced by the Soviet space exploration successes, and in particular the spectacular launch of Sputnik. Thus, there was a great swing in American education towards a scientific/ biological approach to all aspects of education. In physical education, this meant placing emphasis on the biomechanical and physiological aspects of performance; conversely, sport became a laboratory for the analysis of human movement (Demers 1988: 164–5; Macintosh et al. 1987b: 38–9). Indeed, the concept of a unique body of knowledge which could support a new discipline, the science of human movement, had been postulated at the University of California at Berkeley by Franklin Henry in the 1950s. This discipline concept, with its emphasis on science, held great sway over many young faculty members who populated Canadian departments and faculties of physical education in the 1960s and 1970s and, thus, greatly influenced the curricula in these units (cf. also Ingham 1985: 52–3).

At the same time, these departments and faculties of physical education were breaking their traditional ties with colleges and faculties of education and were attempting to make their own way in the mainstream of Canadian universities. As such, they were anxious to establish academic credibility within their respective institutions. What better way than to embrace a "science of human movement"? But not only did these departments and faculties of physical education have to establish academic credibility within their own institutions, it was essential for them to do so as well with the government agencies and peer-review bodies that provided research funds (Demers 1988: 165). Initially, then, the nature of the "new" physical educators' graduate education meant that the most obvious and lucrative source of research funding lay in the pursuit of questions related to health and biological science. These continue to be important for the sport sciences.

It is clear, however, that the Canadian government's decision in the early 1970s to promote and support high-performance sport helped to legitimize research that focused directly on elite athlete performance. It opened up a host of opportunities for scientists working in biomechanics, exercise physiology, and sport psychology, and, indeed, facilitated the development of new specialties (e.g., exercise biochemistry). It is not surprising, then, as Macintosh et al. (1987b) observe, that university physical educators were among the early proponents of the growth of the Canadian "sport system." Neither is it surprising that the "disciplines" and professional languages that constitute the sport sciences address the pushing back of the frontiers of human performance in an unproblematic manner. Indeed, many sport scientists consider this as one of their major *raisons d'être* and use it as an indicator of their "progress" (cf. Beamish 1982; Demers 1988).

These developments were further accelerated by the surplus of teachers which developed as a result of a decline in the school population across Canada which began in the early 1970s. Because of the proliferation of departments and faculties of physical education in the 1960s and because graduates of these programs had traditionally aimed at careers in secondary schools, this teacher surplus had a traumatic impact. Many faculties and departments of physical education embraced the "discipline" concept, extolling the virtue of the study of human movement as a legitimate end in itself. Thus, they could promote their undergraduate curriculum as a worthwhile endeavour in the same manner as did proponents of undergraduate programs in the more traditional arts and sciences disciplines (Macintosh 1986). Alternatively, they sought to prepare their graduates for new professional roles, and to promote the value of these newly constituted kinds of expertise among potential clientele. Typically, these new discourses have traded either on the health sciences connection (e.g., fitness and "wellness" consulting, "lifestyle counselling"), or on the connection with high-performance sport (i.e., in coaching or sport management), especially as management jobs began to open up in the provinces as well as at the federal level. In each of these cases, university sport scientists and researchers have been understandably prominent in articulating the public case for these new forms of knowledge and these new professional roles for their graduates.

Both the "discipline" concept and the search for new professional roles have together reinforced the movement towards a science-based undergraduate curriculum in physical education. They have also created divisions within physical education, pitting the sport scientists (including sport management researchers) against the traditional physical educators and others who have shared a concern with the role of physical activity in the total development of the person (cf. Demers 1988; Lawson 1985). One division is clearly around what Boileau (1982) has termed "sportism" – the preoccupation of these reconstructed departments with sport and, indeed, with high-performance sport. This has been at the expense of the experiential dimensions of sport, at the expense of other modes of physical activity (e.g., dance, outdoor pursuits), and at the expense of the social and philosophical discussions that were a part of physical *education*.

This division between a new "science" of human movement and older social, philosophical, and experiential dimensions of physical activity connects with a deeper, although not always clearly articulated, division about what are the most appropriate knowledge structures for the discipline and the profession (cf. Lawson 1985; Sparks 1985). The sport scientists and "performance technocrats" (ibid.) promote a positivist, technically oriented knowledge structure which seeks to map the way to increased levels of achievement in high-performance sport. Research in the sport sciences pushes back the frontiers of physical and technical performance while social science becomes focused on athlete selection instruments, behaviour management, and the management of organizational change. Beamish (1982) can, therefore, point out that "Of the 131 articles published in the *Canadian Journal of Applied Sport Science* from 1979 to 1981, 73% dealt with material that would directly enhance linear sport ... An additional 13% of the articles presented material that would indirectly contribute to athletic performance" (ibid., 10). The antagonists of the sport sciences – a shifting coalition encompassing physical educators, philosophers, and some historians and sociologists – promote a more critical model of scholarship, capable of posing social and ethical questions about high-performance sport. They also seek to raise a more general set of questions concerning the social relations within which various physical activities have become institutionalized, and, conversely, the role of these institutions in the reproduction and transformation of social relations (cf., for example, Gruneau 1983; Hall 1987; Harvey 1983; Whitson 1984). We say more about this struggle in the final chapter.

However, the fact that critical scholarship in physical education is today on the defensive in university units that are increasingly restructuring themselves as sport science departments points to several developments which are related to the increasing pressures that post-secondary institutions are coming under from governments to justify themselves in utilitarian terms (cf. Aronowitz and Giroux 1985; Connell 1983). First, these forces produce pressures that are felt, especially in less-established faculties and disciplines, to be responding to changes in the job market such as those described above. In part, this is appropriate, of course, but Connell comments on the positive enthusiasm of some academics "to construct new empires in the spaces thus opened up" (ibid., 242). His comments refer generally to the movement of Australian colleges of education into the newer "service-professions" (his example, indeed, is recreation), but they could equally describe the growth of the sport sciences (including sport management programs) in Canadian university education. Indeed, Hardy (1987) describes sport management as a growth industry in American colleges and universities.

At the same time, there is also pressure to make the content of such new courses (and, indeed, existing courses) more applied, more skill-focused, more specifically oriented to prepare graduates for the roles they will be expected to fill in the private sector and in government (again confirmed by Hardy's account of the content of American courses). This, as Aronowitz and Giroux (1985) suggest, means less critical scholarship. Finally, the pressure on academics to generate externally funded research combines with the availability of funding for applied research on high-performance sport to reorient the academic interests of many faculty, and may ultimately reshape their own understandings of what their discipline is about.

Together, all of these factors become part of the context of what Bucher and Strauss (1961) have described as the political jockeying that goes on inside professions as different interest groups and proponents of different epistemological paradigms vie to define the professions' mission (cited in Lawson 1985). In physical education, they have combined to reproduce what Aronowitz and Giroux (1985) refer to as the "technicist tendency" in North American undergraduate and professional programs. This involves an emphasis on technical and management skills and a corresponding deemphasis on the liberal arts subjects that might encourage analysis and questioning of the social relations within which professional skills are applied. It is in just this way that the sport sciences produce managers and researchers and coaches and therapists who know a lot about "organizational needs" or, as Ingham (1985) puts it, "the biological and psychodynamic individual," but very little about the socio-economic and political structures that are the social context of their work (ibid., 51). This despite Drucker's contention (1974) that managers, as opposed to technicians, need to be aware of the social impact of their institution's activities, and to consider questions of social responsibility. If Drucker is correct, it is doubtful whether many sport management and administration courses produce graduates who are adequately prepared for management roles. This is precisely the context of Hardy's call (1987) for a renewed place for the liberal arts in sport management curricula, and for sociological and historical scholarship within the context of sports studies.

Ingham (1985) suggests that the current shift towards management-oriented study and towards kinesiological science, a shift which is manifest to him in his role as a reviewer for several important physical education journals, both reflects and reinforces a new wisdom which disparages the welfare state and seeks to undo the effects of the brief ascendancy of intellectual discourses that had encouraged discussion of *political* responses to the common personal problems of modern life. In locating his contention more concretely, Ingham argues that the physical education profession, in its rush to embrace the fitness movement in North America, has been an unwitting ally of the new conservative Right that has manifested itself in Western industrialized nations in the 1980s. The picture of the "fit" individual in today's society is one who has assumed the responsibility for his or her own health; this focuses attention on individual responsibility and away from the state's responsibility for attending to the health needs of society. For the individuals who do not aspire to or attain this new desired level of physical fitness and for those individuals who are in or who fall into poor health, there is the implication that they have somehow failed themselves.

Ingham's point (ibid.) is not that the new discourses are explicitly political; indeed, he notes that positivist social science strives to present itself as "value-free" (cf. also Beamish 1982; Whitson 1978). Rather it is precisely the ethical and political issues that are left out that are important, the structured silences of an approach to scholarship which takes institutional purposes as presupposed and which "favours the analysis of personal factors and discourages the analysis of social factors" (Ingham 1985: 53). Ingham here is criticizing the discourses of "lifestyle reform" and "stress-management" as responses to the health care debates of the 1980s. But our interviews suggest that the same structured silences in their education have helped to construct the assumptions that many sport management professionals bring to issues of regional and gender inequality, for example, and, indeed, to the way they see their own role in Canadian sport. Together these examples underline the importance of Connell's point (1983) that, when many of the emerging "service professionals" find work in the public sector, it is crucial that their education introduce them to the political and ethical issues which are the background to debates about the welfare state.

III   CONCLUSIONS

We have argued that language plays an important role in the "professionalization project" as a new profession endeavours to construct a place for itself and its knowledge. At the same time, we have argued (cf. Larson 1984) that the emergence and ascendancy of particular discourses can never be disconnected from the power of the institutions which sponsor them and put them into practice. At a general level, this allows us to connect Habermas's account of the development of new academic specialties (cited at the beginning of the chapter) with Rorty's (1979) observation that much of what gets defined as "knowledge" in a society can be read simply as those beliefs and modes of practice which are successful in helping official groups in that society do what they want to do (ibid., 10). With specific reference to the reconstruction of physical education around the discourses of sport sciences, including sport management, we pointed to a conjuncture of the interests of governments in Canada with those of influential groups within university physical education departments and the national and provincial sport organizations themselves. Indeed, their collaboration in the construction of a new discourse and a new knowledge base around high-performance sport stands as an illustration of Lawson's (1985) reminder that a profession's knowledge claims are inevitably constructed with reference to its "missions," missions which are themselves related to definitions of human needs and purposes which "change as they are contested by society's members" (ibid., 21).

We also developed the theme that discourse is important in the construction of professionals themselves; young sport professionals learn to see themselves as scientists and/or managers in large part as a result of the ideas they are exposed to, and crucially *not* exposed to, in the course of their professional preparation. Here, Aronowitz and Giroux's claim (1985) that much of what is called professional education consists in ideological initiation is spelled out more explicitly in Mercer's contention (1984) that "undergraduate students, postgraduates and full-time academics in any given field are painstakingly initiated not only into certain methodological practices and theories relating to their discipline but ... much more importantly, they also tend to take on a particular set of fairly blinkered stereotyped attitudes and ways of looking at the world" (ibid., 159).

In the model of "professionality" that now dominates Canadian physical education, the young sport scientist or sport manager is encouraged to see his or her job as the production of performance (individual or organizational performance) and is seldom seriously introduced to the social and political questions that surround the concentration of resources on elite sport. Sport science is constructed unproblematically as the science of improvement of human performance and physical well-being, while the results-oriented manager is someone who has learned to reformulate human and ethical questions as questions of organizational effectiveness. The technician and the manager alike take "presupposed system goals" for granted; other issues are reduced to a matter of what works, what assists the organization in accomplishing its goals most effectively (MacIntyre 1981: 29).

It is fundamental, moreover, to the "process of formation" of the technocratic professional that (s)he learn not to see this posture as violating ethical norms. It is precisely this framing of human questions in purely technical terms that "liberates decent men (and women) from qualms" (Berlin 1972: 55). Some have sought to proclaim professionalism itself as a value system which establishes the "primacy of cognitive rationality" (cf. Parsons 1968). But we believe that Habermas (1971: 112) is correct in maintaining that this technocratic consciousness is simply a world view in which ethical and political issues are submerged in a calculus of technical and economic rationality. It is not that unethical behaviour is sanctioned or justified, but rather that, when system goals are taken for granted, the "rightness" of practices which can be shown to produce increased system effectiveness becomes difficult to challenge.

To effectively reshape and broaden this results-oriented view, we should remember (cf. Freidson 1984: 24) that only a part of any kind of professional work is technical rather than social and moral, and that professionals who genuinely desire to serve their societies need to understand these distinctions themselves, to work to encourage public understanding of them, and to acknowledge their accountability to lay control. More specifically, sport scientists and managers need to understand where the rationalized pursuit of high performance collides with the equity-related objectives of governments (cf. chap. 7), and that it is essential for them to raise these issues for discussion with elected, regionally representative bodies in their sports. This requires that these sport scientists and managers have an appreciation of the place of these lay bodies in the institution that is Canadian sport, rather than working to depoliticize important policy questions by presenting them as technical questions.

For such a change to take place, however, it is necessary that university physical education programs include exposure to ways of thinking that do not take the value of high-performance sport for granted and to languages which construct other versions of human purposes. Thinking differently requires some exposure to alternative discourses, which allow us the possibility of making new connections and envisioning different roles for ourselves. This is why it is important that university physical education reconstruct a place for the humanities and for scholarship that is alert to the effects of sport in society and is cognizant of questions that are simply not raised when improvements in performance are celebrated uncritically. If the function of the university is not only to train experts in a technical sense but to prepare them to play leadership roles in society, it is crucial that they be encouraged to think critically about the limits of their own knowledge structures. We elaborate on this theme in the final chapter.

CHAPTER TEN

Summing Up

I INTRODUCTION

Our study of the policy-making process in six national sport organizations (NSOs) led us to matters of social concern for the practice of sport in Canada today, concerns that also intersected with political and social issues in Canadian society at large. In this chapter, we return to these concerns and advance some proposals as to how some of the related problems may be ameliorated.

We begin by reiterating the significance of Thompson's (1984) observation (cited in chapter 2) that discourses are not only linguistic but ideological constructs and, therefore, that the impact of new discourses is related not only to their persuasive powers but also to the power of the institutions that sponsor and diffuse them. We are directed, in other words, to the conjunctures of interests that underlie the production and consumption of new forms of knowledge, i.e., new specialties in science and social science (cf. Connell 1983: chap. 13; Demers 1988; Johnston and Robbins 1977; Mercer 1984).

We have argued that the creation of a Canadian high-performance sport system – complete with a large and growing professional bureaucracy, four-year plans, a cadre of state-supported athletes, and a strong commitment to sport sciences – is the result of a conjuncture of the interests of three key "modernizing" groups: one in the sport community itself; a second in government; and a third in the physical education profession. The self-interests of the sport community, or at least of those within it whose preoccupation has always been winning, we have considered to be self-evident. What we explore at greater length in this chapter is the interests of government and the physical education profession in charting the particular course Canada has followed.

II GOVERNMENT

In earlier chapters, we addressed the history of Canadian government involvement in sport and considered various explanations of the growing government presence. In chapter 3, we summarized Macintosh et al.'s analysis (1987b) of successive policy statements, ministerial speeches, and other documents. These offered considerable support for an analysis that emphasizes the political mileage Canadian governments have sought in identifying themselves with the promotion of Canadian success in international sport events, events that television has turned into world festivals. Successive administrations have seen successes in international sport as a way of promoting identification with the Canadian nation, of instilling a sense of nationalistic pride among Canadians, and, not incidentally, encouraging people to identify these successes with the government of the day. Nationalism is a language that organizes "we-they" identifications around the nation state. Goldlust (1987) has pointed out that sport has offered a way of mobilizing group solidarity against a common foe that has proved attractive to many different kinds of government (cf. also Hoberman 1984). We argued, however, that the Canadian government took an increasingly directive role in order to try to see that success in international sport events was achieved.

In chapter 7, we summarized evidence developed in chapters 5 and 6 that suggested that the Canadian government's increasing commitment to international success, as manifest in the creation of Sport Canada and the growth of an increasingly sophisticated sport system, was producing regular and systematic conflicts with other official goals of Canadian social policy. These social goals included commitments to reducing regional inequities, to equalizing opportunities for women and for francophones, and to improving access to cultural and recreational opportunities among low-income Canadians. All of these equity-oriented objectives are explicitly mentioned in sport policy documents; gender equity, in particular, is formally promoted by Sport Canada. Yet we noted in our interviews that these kinds of goals were routinely subordinated to what was seen as the "real" job of NSOs: constructing programs that would produce more medal-winners in international games. Officials clearly feel this pressure, just as athletes do, and it is one of our central themes that, in the mind-set that now dominates Sport Canada at every level, equity is clearly less important than high-performance goals.

In an effort to explain these tensions between equity and high-performance goals, our analysis turned to the purposes of government involvement in sport from both comparative and theoretical points of view. We compared the Canadian experience and the Sport Canada model with the rather different history and mandate of the Sports Council in the United Kingdom. Then we used these comparisons and contrasts to introduce debates about the proper role of government in the economy and in traditionally non-political institutions like sport. We next considered whether opportunities to participate in sport were an extension of social rights (i.e., part of equity-oriented social programs), or alternatively, whether the international successes of Canadian elites (in this case, high-performance athletes) could be considered objectives that served the public interest.

We suggested that the Canadian state's support for high-profile international sport creates potential opportunities for some groups in the business sector: moreover, that this endeavour is generally consistent with the dominant meanings and values of a meritocratic and competitive society. At the same time, we argued that the state's involvement in highly visible areas of popular culture that clearly provide some opportunities for members of disadvantaged groups to succeed (however exceptional they may be) helps the state to legitimate itself to the public. However, we also suggested that in neither case was the demand or need for high-performance sport sufficient to warrant a conclusion that the Canadian state's current preoccupation with high performance reflects entirely either economic or political necessity. We must look as well to the projects of particular interest groups. It is in this light that we need to consider briefly how proposals for the further integration of a Canadian sport development system are complicated by the size and variety of the country, by the competing claims of different regional interests and the national interest, and by federal-provincial jurisdictional divisions.

In chapter 5, we documented the struggle in NSOs between those who championed regional programs and athlete development (usually volunteer executive members from outside central Canada) and those who argued for a centralization of services and facilities in order to prepare high-performance athletes for international competitions (usually professional staff members and volunteer executive members from large metropolitan cities and south-western Ontario). We concluded chapter 5 by noting that this was a struggle that was being fought out over other issues in Canada, such as excellence in higher education and free trade, and with similar results. The outcome of this struggle in sport has taken NSOs towards a more centralized and rationalized structure, in which decisions were made on the basis of information provided by professional staff members and by volunteer executive members selected on the basis of their expertise rather than by region. One of the impacts of this change certainly has been to focus more of the resources of NSOs on the development of high-performance athletes and to centralize these resources in "centres of excellence," typically located in large metropolitan cities in Ontario and in certain large cities in the "have" provinces. The purpose of this centralization of resources has been to bring promising young athletes from around the country to centres (e.g., at the University of Toronto or the University of Calgary) where they can train under national coaches and have access to the best in facilities and sport sciences support.

Such centres of excellence play an important role, just as do their counterparts in Eastern Europe, in the development of the young athlete from "promise" to "accomplishment." They offer the concrete opportunities outlined above. But they also induct the young athlete more fully into the culture of high-performance sport and mark a transition, for many, from the semi-serious world of school sport to the full-time commitment expected of the state athlete. Yet, they also draw attention to gaps – in expectation and commitment, as well as performance – between the good junior and the international athlete. Efforts to bridge these gaps, moreover, inevitably point to questions of mandate and jurisdiction, with national and provincial sport organizations, schools and universities all having different ideas about their own responsibilities and those of their partners.

The question of jurisdiction in sport is a matter that has been brought on a number of occasions to the agenda of the interprovincial sport and recreation ministers' council. This organization has met many times over the past twenty-five years, ostensibly to rationalize and coordinate the roles of the respective levels of government in sport and recreation. Indeed, in its national sport policy document, *Toward 2000*, the federal government listed as one of its eight national goals the establishment of a "coherent Canadian Sport System" (Canada 1988: 77).The most feasible way for such a national plan to work within the framework of Canadian federalism would be to assign to the NSOs (supported by Sport Canada) the role of supporting the country's elite international athletes, with provincial sport organizations (supported by the respective provinces) responsible for developmental programs for promising young athletes in their own jurisdictions, as well as for mass sport and recreation programs. In this way, the roles of the respective levels of government would complement rather than duplicate each other.

This rationalization of the proper role of the two levels of government in sport, however, has never come about. Instead, there has been a tendency for some provinces (especially the "have" provinces) to reproduce the same emphasis on high-performance sport that we have described in the NSOs, with the same neglect of community and recreational sport. Provinces compete to place members on national teams and to place highly in Canada Games standings; provincial sport organization staff are under the same sort of performance-driven pressures that we have described at length at the national level, and with similar results.

Harvey (1983) has described the ambitions of the Quebec state of the 1970s in this respect. British Columbia now relates funding of its sport organizations to their success in Canada Games. More recently, Laurin (1988) has described how the effect of Alberta's Sport Development Policy has been to focus the efforts of provincial sport organizations on elite performance and to reproduce similar organizational changes to those that have characterized the NSOs in Ottawa (cf. also Slack and Hinings 1987b, for a discussion of this trend). At the same time as the larger, more prosperous provinces are pushing forward with programs for the high-performance athletes in their jurisdictions, the "have not" provinces do not have the population base or the resources to carry out this mandate. The result has been similar to those in other jurisdictions in today's federal-provincial struggles over the disposition of shrinking tax revenues and jurisdictional disputes; there are substantial inequalities in opportunities for young Canadians to develop their talents in sport according to the region of the country in which they live.

It is ironic that some provinces have taken this stance, because in the early years of the Fitness and Amateur Sport Act, they championed mass sport and recreation programs and jealously guarded their jurisdictional rights in this domain, to the extent that the federal government terminated the federal-provincial cost-sharing agreements in fitness and amateur sport in the late 1960s. This propensity on the part of the provinces also attests to the current dominance of the high-performance model of sport in Canada and to the extent to which the professional world-view of sport has influenced the practice of sport at all levels of skill and competition.

It is equally ironic that the federal government, after years of pushing NSOs to focus their efforts on the development of international-calibre athletes, has apparently finally seen that this thrust has resulted in a neglect of domestic sport programs. Witness the statement in the 1988–92 Quadrennial Planning and Evaluation Guide (Fitness and Amateur Sport 1988) urging the NSOs to think again about domestic development and about the provision of opportunities "for those who participate in sport for its own sake and ... who may not have the aspiration to excel at the international level" (ibid., 9). Some who remember federal government rhetoric in previous white papers about support for mass sport programs may wish to see more concrete examples of commitment of funds for this purpose before they are convinced of the conviction of this most recent federal government exhortation.

Such scepticism seems all the more warranted in light of suggestions in *Toward 2000* that sport programs in schools and universities be integrated more closely with the performance-oriented sport system. Phrased in the language of "Sport System Meets School System" (Canada 1988), this is unexceptional. Indeed, it appears to promise many of the things we advocate: support for fitness programs and the teaching of "core" sports in the elementary schools; skills coaching packages designed for use in high schools and community centres. However, we are alerted by suggestions by assistant deputy minister Lyle Makosky, in the wake of the 1988 Seoul Olympics, that we need to start youngsters into high-performance-oriented instruction and practice at an earlier age, and by suggestions by one of our own respondents that Canadian universities (and even metropolitan area high schools) who take sport seriously should form "super leagues" at their respective levels, which would serve as development leagues for the national program. These views serve as apt reminders that the needs of the student-athlete are not necessarily the same as those of the high-performance sport system.

Canadian educational institutions, including both secondary and post-secondary levels, have, by and large, sustained a consensus that sport exists within the school system because of its educational value. The purposes of school sport have been educational and recreational, rather than to develop elite or professional athletes. Indeed, in some sports (e.g., hockey) physical educators have consciously distanced their programs from club programs when they perceived that the latter were too intense and performance-oriented to coexist easily with the aims of education. We believe that very few Canadians are attracted either to the "sport school" model of Eastern Europe or the different but still performance-oriented system of many American high schools and universities. The tradition of education through physical activity is richly varied in Canada, incorporating ethnic and modern dance as well as non-competitive sport, recreational, and wilderness activities. It also very properly emphasizes the value of physical activities for the less skilled. We oppose very strongly, therefore, any suggestion that physical education move to a greater emphasis on sports skills, especially in younger age groups. Provincial education authorities will need to be very careful in meetings with advocates of the high-performance sport system, and think very carefully about what interests are served in proposals that Canadian physical education curricula be adapted to the needs of a national sport development system.

Indeed, Canadians may well want to consider a diminished rather than an expanded role for the federal government in Canadian sport. Whether or not it proves more difficult in a post–Meech Lake political climate for federal governments to mount any kind of new national programs (cf. Banting 1987: chap. 11), it is hard to imagine that provinces will not remain very sensitive to any hint of interference in their jurisdiction over education, or that they will consider high-performance sport so much in the national interest as to transcend this perennial federal-provincial squabble.

Our concerns should not be read as a plea to reduce federal government spending on sport. We believe that sport is important in the lives of many Canadians, and, indeed, that government should help provide opportunities for talented individuals to reach their full potential in sport just as it does in other areas of Canadian culture. We consider, moreover, that only federal funding can help to equalize access to cultural opportunities. Without federal funding, the differences in provincial and municipal tax bases can only mean that inequities will widen instead of diminish. What we do advocate is that such funding be channelled through some genuinely arm's-length agency, as it is through the Canada Council in the case of the arts. We are under no illusions that such agencies entirely satisfy the interests of regions, or of others not aligned with dominant ideologies. We consider, nonetheless, that the politics of such bodies produces more diversity and more sensitivity to minority aspirations than decision structures that are more constructed by the world views of senior professional staff and politicians. A more radical view, which has gained some support since the Dubin drug inquiry of 1988–89, is that the federal and provincial governments should get entirely out of the promotion of high-performance sport and focus their efforts on assisting local governments and agencies in the fostering of "sport-for-all" programs.

In *Toward 2000* (Canada 1988), recommendations were made that would go some way towards alleviating the currect imbalance of power in national sport policy making. The task force recommended that the National Fitness and Amateur Sport Advisory Council be abolished and replaced by a *Consultative* Council on National Sport (emphasis ours). In the critical area of Fitness and Amateur Sport Branch accountability to Parliament, however, the task force could come to no agreement, but did suggest that "the idea merited further examination" (ibid., 71). The issue of a quasi-independent National Sport Council, along the lines of the Canada Council, with its own administrative arm, Sport Canada, was not broached in the report. We see this latter step as being crucial to distancing national sport policy making from the political whims of the day and from domination by strong ministers and senior public servants (cf. Macintosh et al. 1987b, chap. 10, for an elaboration of these proposals).

III PROFESSIONALIZATION

What may be more important in the long run in democratizing national sport policy making, however, is that it be reclaimed from the new sport professionals. This can best be accomplished on two fronts: first, through policy-making structures that include representatives of participants and users whose "presupposed system goal" may not be the production of performance, and policy processes that encourage real public input; and second, through debates about the meanings and values Canadians identify with in sport (and how much we are prepared to change in order to achieve international success).

In chapter 4, we set the stage for the issues discussed in chapters 5, 6, and 7 by examining the process of professionalization of the people who were hired to manage and direct the affairs of the NSOs once the National Sport and Recreation Centre (NSRC) was established in Ottawa by the federal government in 1970. We discussed the power struggles that have historically attended the establishment of new professions. We elaborated as well on the nature of the ideological work professionals had to do and the epistemological claims they had to make in order to both popularize and privilege their particular form of knowledge. We suggested that the establishment of a new professional bureaucracy at the NSRC is an instance of precisely these sorts of dynamics, in which aspirant professions have articulated new knowledge in the sport sciences and management with the aspirations of significant groups in the sports themselves and in government. In this way, they have succeeded in diminishing the influence of those who have been stewards of other meanings and values in Canadian sport.

We also argued in chapter 9 that departments and faculties of physical education in Canadian universities played no small role in this professionalization of the national and provincial sport bureaucracies. They have done so by promoting professional qualifications in sport science and sport management as a desirable, even necessary, qualification for employment in national and provincial sport organizations and government departments of recreation, fitness, and sport. That this professionalization also provided new employment opportunities for graduates of university physical education programs at a time when the traditional market, secondary school teaching, was drying up, and that it also helped to establish the new university discipline of sport sciences as a vital part of the training of high-performance athletes, should come as no surprise. Indeed, Harvey and Proulx's account (1988) of the role of Quebec university physical educators on the Belisle commission in creating new professional roles in sport and recreation in the new Quebec (cited in chap. 9) is a story that, in our view, could be replicated in any histories of the development of many provincial sport and fitness and recreation departments across Canada, and indeed, at the national level.

What is important here, first, is that the formation and implementation of sport policy, and the ways in which sport policies reinforce or conflict with other policy objectives, will in practice reflect the understandings of the purposes of sport (and of national and provincial sport organizations) that are shared by those who are present at successive levels of decision making. This is precisely why it has mattered that the extension of the concept of the rights of citizens to sport and recreation opportunities was accompanied by the establishment of "professional cultures" (Harvey and Proulx 1988: 109), in which new kinds of experts defined individual and societal needs as well as optimal ways of satisfying them.

Second, it matters how these new sport experts have learned to understand the nature and purposes of their particular knowledge. We have maintained, following Lawson (1984), that the knowledge claims of the physical educator have been radically transformed, until the new disciplines associated with "human kinetics" are no longer about the education of human beings through physical activity. Instead, they are primarily about the systematic and scientific production of athletic performance (cf. also Demers 1988, on "sportism"). As a result, Canadian sport scientists and managers have formulated the production of sport performance as a series of technical and organizational challenges. They also tend to see their relative mastery of the technical issues (relative to volunteers) as justifying their own ascendancy within the Canadian sport system, and increasingly, their effective control of policy and planning structures.

This ascendancy of sport managers and scientists is spelled out in *Toward 2000* in the task force's explicit commitment: "To enhance the legitimacy and funding of the essential professions (coaching, sport science, sport administration, sport medicine, etc.) required to develop and sustain an effective high performance system" (Canada 1988: 36). In an earlier passage it is also considered important "To revise the responsibilities for policy formulation ... with professional staff providing primary leadership to the process of policy development and implementation" (ibid., 32). Indeed, "organizational development" is virtually equated with this reversal of the roles of volunteers and paid staff, something which we discussed in chapter 4.

It needs to be remembered that professionals seldom acknowledge that this "rationalization" of policy-making structures is something that institutionalizes their own power. We observed in chapters 2 and 4 that professionals themselves are normally completely sincere in their advocacy of the social value of their knowledge. For a considerable time, the orthodox view was to see professionalism itself as a progressive social development, and professionals as agents of progress. Indeed, "The idea that professional experts were disinterested was the central tenet of the Progressive faith, and it was precisely because experts were so perceived that the great expansion of their authority during the early decades of this century could seem to pose no threat to the public interest" (Haskell 1984: xxix). Yet, the very confidence of professionals' conviction that they know best (a confidence that is not unique to the sport professionals under discussion here) raises a series of questions that warrant exploration. The most important of these is the one formulated by Habermas (1971) and Offe (1984) as "depoliticization" (see chap. 4 for this discussion and the citations).

At a general level, depoliticization is accomplished when many kinds of questions that have political and normative implications (like all of the equity issues raised in chaps. 5 through 7) are represented as technical questions. The range of issues that lay people are encouraged to understand and debate and pass judgment upon is sharply diminished. Thus, the political process and ultimately public life itself are impoverished (cf. also Forester 1985 and Haskell 1984, for discussions of specific instances). At the concrete level of specific sport organizations, depoliticization is accomplished when the rationalization of decision-making structures means that those who would represent different interests (e.g., of regions or of francophones), let alone different visions of institutional purposes, can be effectively frozen out. The reconstruction of NSO committees on the basis of expertise rather than political representation is a clear instance of this depoliticization of decision making. Participation in policy making is restricted to those who agree on ends, and who are unlikely to persist in raising issues that complicate the pursuit of those ends. Again, there is a clear tension between "efficient" policy processes and ones that are either democratic or empowering for subordinate groups (cf. Forester 1985).

It is instructive to extend this tension between "efficiency" and "democracy" in policy making to the notion of "management" as a specific body of technical knowledge. Abby Hoffman, director-general of Sport Canada through most of the 1980s, was known to be concerned that many Canadian university undergraduate degrees in physical education, kinesiology, and related fields do not prepare their graduates well for positions in such areas of sport administration as management, fund raising, and publicity. Certainly, the job requirements of executive positions in Canadian NSOs today place a premium on skills and experience in these specific areas. However, we have been critical in chapter 9 of "management" as a discourse that takes system goals for granted, whether these are the production of goods or sport performance. This constructs a role for managers as those who organize human and material resources so as to achieve these goals in the most cost-effective manner. In the current environment, this view has increasingly emphasized revenue production and financial controls. Our point is simply that an understanding of financial management should be accompanied by an understanding of the political economy in which public provision exists. No one would deny that it is incumbent upon all those working in the public services to seek cost-effective means of service delivery, or that careful planning and operational management are not important, if finite resources are to be deployed to the greatest public benefit. At the same time, we must also insist that public services embody goals and purposes that are different from those of corporations. These public service purposes have to do with equity and with the development of individuals and communities, and can never be automatically subordinated to economic calculations, if the "public services" are to retain any of their original meanings.

We return to the task-oriented and uncritical nature of much that passes for professional training in many other fields as well as our own. Bender (1984) reminds us that an earlier generation of intellectuals like Snow and Whitehead expressed concern that the education of the new knowledge-based elites was becoming too narrowly focused. Yet he suggests that the situation is even worse today. Bender remarks that "the academic disciplines in America have been astonishingly successful in producing new knowledge," but at the cost of producing "island communities" who cannot talk to each other, let alone inform a public debate about the uses and abuses of new forms of specialist knowledge (ibid., 100–1). Closer to home, similar concerns were voiced at a national conference sponsored by the Social Sciences Foundation of Canada, which was held in Ottawa in October 1988. Howard Clark, president of Dalhousie University, summed up the feelings of the delegates by stating that what is "at stake is the university's ability to 'educate' in the face of 'compelling pressures' to specialize in almost every discipline" (*Ottawa Citizen*, 3 Oct. 1988:

A10). What is raised here, of course, relates to the nature of the education of the new sport professionals. In particular, to what extent has the reconstruction of physical education, described in chapter 8, meant the reduction or even elimination of the very courses in the humanities and critical social sciences that could acquaint aspiring sport professionals with political theory and with ethical frameworks that could take them beyond technical reason?

We pointed out in chapter 9 that the science of human movement became the core of undergraduate programs that used to be known as physical education but now more often carry names such as kinesiology, sport sciences, and human movement studies. The scientific base of these new programs replaced the old pedagogy and practical physical activity courses that constituted the core of the curriculum for the preparation of the traditional physical education teacher. But in this process, many programs also did away with the philosophy and issues courses that alerted students to the fact that there were larger ethical and social implications involved in "physically educating" young people. Indeed, in the rush by the old physical education units to embrace the science of human movement, many of those faculty members who were interested in the social sciences also sought to establish a "scientific" base for their work, where scientific meant modelled on the methods of the natural sciences. Thus, they were also quick to pursue research that was of a quantitative rather than qualitative nature, and to proclaim the "value-free" nature of this work. Physical education was not alone in this, of course; many of the social sciences succumbed for a time to these positivist pressures. In most social sciences, however, the critique of the limits of positivism is today widely accepted. But as a result of this rush to embrace science by university physical education departments, most of the academic journals in which university sport scientists now publish are almost devoid of any discussion of social issues or philosophical or ethical questions.

The result is that there is little questioning in these new departments of kinesiology/sport sciences of the validity or the underlying ethics of the science of human movement. It was the writings and speeches of the grand old men of physical education, such as Pat Galasso, Gerry Glassford, John Meagher, and Earle Zeigler, who had a vision of the generalist physical educator, that helped keep alive the ethical and philosophical issues in physical education. It is also worth noting that in Great Britain, a separate women's tradition in physical education persisted into the 1970s. This tradition was characterized not only by its own distinctive activities but also by an ethos that emphasized the educative value of expressive physical activities. Fletcher (1984) describes, however, how in the recent rationalization of British higher education, this women's tradition has been subordinated to a male one which emphasizes the scientific production of performance.

Whatever one thinks of the relevance of the traditional visions of the purposes of physical education, we sorely miss people who would raise moral and ethical and philosophical questions about present-day practices in sport and physical activity programs. Graduates of new kinesiology/sport sciences/sport management programs usually leave the university without realizing that the application of the scientific method to problem solving always involves an investigator bias and almost always has underlying social and ethical ramifications (cf. Beamish 1982; Martens 1987; Whitson 1978). When their education has downplayed and even excluded the study of social and philosophical issues, it is scarcely surprising that the new Canadian sport bureaucracy has not been active in the defence of "sport for all" or much concerned with equity or ethical issues.

We see few signs in Canadian universities that there will be any change in this scientific, positivist bent towards the study of human movement. Politically, these new units of kinesiology/sport sciences have aligned themselves with medical and allied health professions and science departments. This applied orientation is consonant with what Aronowitz and Giroux (1985) describe as "the technicist tendency" in North American education (ibid., 197), a way of packaging knowledge that consistently ignores its political implications. Indeed, we foresee that existing courses and programs that focus on philosophical, ethical, and social issues will have a hard time surviving in many university programs in the next decade, much less improve on their already precarious position in the curriculum. The demise at the University of Waterloo in the mid-1980s of one of the only two PH D programs in the sociology of sport in anglophone universities in Canada is one very dramatic example of this trend.

Change, in our view, will have to come from pressure from outside these university departments and outside the national sport structure. There are signs that parents of children who participate in high-performance sport programs in their community clubs, and indeed, in their school sport programs, are raising questions about a system that is preoccupied with performance standards. Such a system leaves the vast majority of competitors, who eventually drop out of competitive sport long before they reach the ranks of Canada's elite athletes, without having sensed or experienced many of the intrinsic and social values that used to be seen as important outcomes of sport for young people. It is such parents, in their contact with local and provincial sport organizations and ultimately with NSOs, who may take the lead in forcing a reexamination of the performance-oriented values of today's dominant form of sport.

With respect to the university and the education/training debate, there is no shortage of voices today who are critical of higher education. On the one hand, there are those who call for education to be even more directly geared to the labour market and to demands for specific kinds of technical knowledge. On the other, there are those who advocate a renewed emphasis on the humanities and liberal arts. Even in the latter case, we distinguish our own agenda from those for whom excellence in a liberal arts education means mastery of a core curriculum of great books (cf. Hirsch 1987). Even more, we distance ourselves from those who consider that critical analysis of philosophical issues can be practiced and developed only among an academically elite student population (cf. Bloom 1987). We believe that the humanities and critical social sciences have an important place in physical education, and, indeed, in all professional education. It is in these subjects that students can encounter and practice the habits of thought that will equip them to analyse the political, economic, and cultural processes that structure Canadian society. It is in these subjects that students can learn to address the ethical implications of technical and economic rationality. They also can learn to see through the structured silences of professional and administrative discourses that deemphasize or ignore such issues (cf. Aronowitz and Giroux 1985). Finally, it is in this environment that young professionals can internalize the habits of critical literacy (including self-criticism). These habits will equip them to make intellectual and ethical appraisals of their own practice, and to integrate that practice with working towards a better and fairer society, and towards a more informed public sphere (cf. Bender 1984; Katz 1982; Sullivan 1986).

IV   EPILOGUE

The difficulty in seeing the ethical issues raised by the production of high-performance athletes was highlighted, of course, by the Ben Johnson affair. On the one hand, we have noted that the minister of state for fitness and amateur sport, Jean Charest, was on record as saying that the Canadian government takes the directive role it does in Canadian sport in part to try to ensure "the ethical conduct of sport." Certainly, the government, Sport Canada, and the Canadian Track and Field Association were swift to establish inquiries and to promise punishment of the guilty.

Yet there is an important sense, noted by former Olympian Bruce Kidd (1988), in which this determination to punish guilty individuals avoided discussion of our collective responsibility for this sort of sorry event. The focus on who did what and knew what in the Dubin inquiry served to deflect attention from the extent to which Ben Johnson and the other Canadian throwers and weight-lifters who had been caught out on drug tests were products of the system we established and the messages we consistently gave them. Certainly, the minister of state for fitness and amateur sport was quick to put in place a Sport Canada drug policy (Fitness and Amateur Sport 1984) after the drug-testing débâcle at the 1984 Pan-American Games in Venezuela and the apprehension shortly thereafter of Canadian weight-lifters with steroids in their possession. But Sport Canada and the Canadian Olympic Association (COA) continued to use international performance standards: Sport Canada to determine who would be funded by the Athlete Assistance Program (AAP), and the COA to decide who would be selected for the 1988 Canadian Olympic team. Canadian athletes who aspired to "A-card" levels of support from the AAP had to place in the top eight performers in the world and in the top sixteen to qualify for the 1988 Olympic team. In events such as weight lifting and in many of the power events in track and field, it was very difficult to meet these standards without using anabolic steroids. The athlete was placed in a Catch-22 position, in which fame and rewards were promised to the winners, while the alternatives were mediocrity and/ or retirement. The revelations that the Soviet Union had disciplined 290 of her athletes for using banned drugs in the three years leading up to the 1988 Olympics (*Globe and Mail*, 29 March 1989: A1); that the United States Olympic Committee had offered "non-punitive" drug-testing services for that country's athletes prior to the 1984 Los Angeles Olympics (Hynes, 29 March 1989); and that the International Amateur Athletics Federation had acted fraudulently at its 1983 World Championships when not a single athlete failed drug tests despite suspicions of widespread use (Hynes, 7 May 1989) make it hard to believe that Sport Canada, the COA, and, indeed, Canadian Track and Field Association officials were not aware of the widespread use of drugs in high-performance sport. "In the state-driven Olympic sport system Canadians have created, opportunities and kudos go exclusively to winners and record breakers ... The old amateur ideal of sport for sport's sake, as a challenging form of self-education, is rarely mentioned, let alone encouraged" (Kidd 1988: D8).

Northrop Frye once remarked that everything a culture produces must be acknowledged as a product of that culture. We cannot pretend that going beyond the rules in order to win (whether it involves drugs, or the use of violence as a tactic in hockey) is not a product of the messages and the reward structures we have established; "all these phenomena are not simply blemishes – they are its outputs. These unpleasing threats to all we hold most dear are products of a system so organized as to produce them – to produce them and not their contraries" (Beer 1974, cited in Nelson 1976: 31).

It is not that Ben Johnson is a victim. Rather, he and his entourage, like the other Canadian athletes who have been suspended for drug offences, are products of a Canadian high-performance sport system whose discourse and reward structures are entirely oriented towards winning. When our senior sport officials say, "But maybe we have to start looking at winning as a far greater part of the goal than participation" (Jack Lynch, technical director, Canadian Olympic Association, interview with James Christie, *Globe and Mail*, 3 Oct. 1988), can we be surprised that our athletes take us seriously? This is especially true when they are also products of a society that increasingly accepts other kinds of cheating (in politics and the business world and in private life), and accepts performance-enhancing drugs in other kinds of workplaces (we are indebted for this point to Andy Higgins, Canadian Decathlon Coach, interviewed on "As It Happens," 3 Oct. 1988).

The answer is not to be found in more sophisticated drug testing or more Draconian penalties, but rather in a more searching look at the system we have created, and at the purposes of public expenditure on sport. Jean Charest maintained that "Canadians want an accessible sport system, but they also want excellence from those at the top end of the system – the country's high performance athletes ... Canadians now know that we can be competitive with the best in the world – and they expect us to do so effectively" (Minister's Overview, Canada 1988: 10). We question whether this is what Canadians want, except perhaps with respect to hockey. Olympic scholar John MacAloon, responding to Taylor's claim (1988) that elite sporting success is a "public good," made the point that while Brazilians go into national despair when their national soccer team loses, the 1988 Olympic successes of 800–metre runner Joachim Cruz created only a mild and temporary stir. The point is not to belittle Cruz's achievements; indeed, they were magnificent. Rather it is that, for better or worse, achievements in the Olympic sports matter more to those who have something at stake — the participants, of course, but also now sport professionals and government — than they do to the public. Indeed, this is acknowledged when Sport Canada deems it necessary to teach the Olympic sports to market themselves to the public, and to promote high-performance sport as a part of Canadian culture (Canada 1988: secs. 2.3.5; 6.3).

The reality is that Canadians are interested in sport. The media attention now given to the Olympic sports allows us to appreciate the excellence of a Pierre Harvey, an Alison Higson, or a Dave Steen. We are happy that we can give them some material support in their quests, described so well by Kidd (1988) as challenging forms of self-education, and we are happy for them and with them when they do well. Yet, the fact that neither of the former two lived up to the expectations of Sport Canada in the 1988 Olympics was less an issue for Canadians than it was for the sport bureaucracy, who apparently felt their own programs were at stake. The rest of us shared the athletes' disappointment; but after a day's headlines we got on with our lives (often including our own recreational participation), just as we did when our soccer team was bounced out of the 1988 World Cup by Guatemala. Indeed, the message of most of those who took the trouble to correspond (with the *Globe and Mail* or the CBC) was not of anger but of sadness. We were sad about Ben Johnson's personal tragedy, but also more generally at how what is good in sport, what we enjoy about sport in our own lives and our own communities, is distorted and corrupted by the clear message of "win or else" (cf., for example, *Globe and Mail*, Letters to the Editor, 1 Oct. 1988: D7).

Sport Canada, as we noted in chapter 7, has set as its objective "To have Canada place among the three leading Western nations (with West Germany and the USA) and to rank among the top 6–8 nations overall in the 1992 Summer Olympic Games in Barcelona" (Canada 1988: sec. 2.2). Most Canadians, however, recognize (like the coach we cited in chapters 4 and 7) that if we want to compete with East Germany and with countries many times our size, we will not only have to devote enormous resources to high-performance sport (cf. Hoberman 1984), resources which can only come from other areas of social expenditure. We will also need to go about the production of high-performance athletes in the ways it is done in those countries that routinely make the top eight, and we will have to subordinate many aspects of Canadian social policy and many aspects of Canadian sport culture to this purpose.

Like the coach, we are not sure that Canadians, outside the intense world of the national sport bureaucracy, want to pay these prices. Unlike him, however, we consider that Canadians are wise in this. Sport Canada and the Canadian government should face the reality that international performance standards – many of which are tainted by the use of performance-enhancing drugs – must be abandoned in favour of a system that sets reasonable standards, based on the Canadian sport environment and Canadian goals, one that takes far more account of the values of self-realization and personal accomplishment in sport and pays far more attention to equity and ethical issues.

Research Procedures

The observations presented in the text derive from a three-dimensional study of policy making in national sport organizations (NSOs), encompassing a survey, document searches, and interviews. The object of the research was the evolving role of professional staff, based in the National Sport and Recreation Centre (NSRC) in Ottawa, in the policy-making processes of Canadian sport. To explore this, we opted in the latter two stages for a case-study approach. This focused on the making of policy with respect to three common issues in the recent history of Canadian sport, in six selected sport organizations.

The choice of a case-study approach to this work deserves some elaboration. Given the nature and scope of our project, it was our belief that an intensive study of a few associations was more likely to be revealing than any attempt to sample a larger number in a more superficial or purely quantitative fashion. Through documentary records and, especially, interviews with participants in policy making in these associations, the intricacies of the interplay between structures and individuals could be better explored. The case study attempts to portray the real complexity of social interactions by representing the nuances of conflicting viewpoints and the dynamics of how these were negotiated and resolved. The case study, moreover, permits generalizations: either about an instance or from an instance to a category or class, so long as the reader is persuaded that the events or tensions described are typical of other similar situations. The subsequent process of critical analysis and theory building, then, is a social process, grounded in the logic of naturalistic inquiry (for a fuller discussion of these issues see Carr and Kemmis 1986; Lincoln and Guba 1985; Stake 1980; Whitson 1976).

The criteria for the selection of the six NSOs for the case-study aspect of our research also deserve a brief comment. First, we wished to involve NSOs that were engaged in an Olympic sport. Second, we wanted sports that had a reasonably high profile in the media. A third criterion was that the NSO should have a substantial level of female participation at the elite level. Finally, we wished to balance the associations according to team and individual sports. The application of these criteria resulted in the selection of the following six sports for our case studies: basketball, canoeing, gymnastics, swimming, track and field, and volleyball. The policy areas we chose to explore – high performance versus mass participation sport programming, increasing opportunities for women in leadership (i.e., executive and coaching) positions, and athletes' rights – were either ones that had been the focus of recent debate and policy formation, or ones where NSOs were being pressed by Sport Canada to develop policy. They also represented areas where Sport Canada was pushing the NSOs to develop "ownership" of these policies through a process of debate, rather than (as in the case of tobacco sponsorship or performance-enhancing drugs) simply laying down the policy itself.

Before proceeding with these case studies, however, we sought certain demographic information about the population who are the "new professionals" in the Canadian sport system. To this end, a questionnaire was developed and, with assistance at the NSRC and Sport Canada, circulated among all the professional staffers – executive and technical directors, national coaches, program and marketing officers, and program consultants – who were employed in the NSOs based at the NSRC in the summer of 1986. We also surveyed sport consultants based in Sport Canada who liaised with the NSOs. This survey elicited information about the age, gender, family background, regional origin, ethnicity, educational qualifications, sport background, and career patterns of this population. The results of this survey form the basis of the remarks we make about the background and qualifications of sport professionals. They also permit comparisons to be made with the population who used to comprise the decision makers in Canadian sport (cf. Beamish 1978; Hollands and Gruneau 1979), and they provide a baseline for assessing the real success of programs to improve, for example, female or francophone representation in high-performance sport.

At the same time, we undertook a search of relevant documents in the six selected NSOs. We were particularly interested in association minutes, agendas, memos, correspondence, Fitness and Amateur Sport policy documents and communiqués, as well as more widely circulated material such as House of Commons debates, newspaper articles, and ministerial statements and speeches. In the case of association documents, some were naturally more complete than others; but in every case we are grateful to NSO staff for making available what they had for our perusal. We looked, for example, for proposals to form women's committees, for evidence of support for (or opposition to) planning initiatives or athlete representation in decision making. Sometimes it was simply the absence of any reference to an issue that appeared noteworthy. We were also looking for who had been the key individuals, both professional and volunteer, in the making of policy in these NSOs. In other words, whose names recurred in shaping policy on particular issues?

In this way we identified the key actors in each sport whom we wished to interview. In each case, we interviewed the incumbent executive direc-tor or equivalent. Sometimes these individuals had not been with the NSOs for long enough to have played a role in the events we were interested in; but they always offered an important glimpse into current thinking, and their cooperation was important in referring us to other staff, past as well as present. Likewise, we sought wherever possible to touch base with the incumbent volunteer president, although in several instances it proved to be much more important to talk to individuals who had held national office at the time the policies we were concerned with had been on the agenda. These people either became evident in the document searches, or they were referred to us as key actors by other interviewees.

Eventually, we conducted fifty-six interviews between October 1986 and April 1987 with individuals who had played some role – whether as professional, volunteer executive member, or Sport Canada consultant – in the relevant policy debates. It is worth noting that, had we restricted ourselves to the most senior personnel, professional or volunteer, our interview subjects would have been almost entirely male. In order to ensure a fair airing of the women's issue, however, we also contacted a number of women whom other interviewees referred to us as having played active roles in their respective sports. On the volunteer side, this meant that we interviewed several former committee members. With respect to professional staff, it led us to several women who had taken executive director positions in other, smaller sport organizations as the most realistic way of furthering their professional careers. In this way, we were able to ensure that one-third of our interviewees were female.

It is also worth noting that because few athletes appeared in our docu-ment searches, and because, with only one exception, athletes' rights was not a serious issue for the people we did interview, this topic was gradually supplanted in our agenda by quadrennial planning. This latter issue was always raised in any discussion of high-performance versus mass sport and almost always generated the most feeling and the most reflection.

The interviews themselves had an "agenda" rather than a fixed set of questions, and although we were broadly interested in the issues indicated above, the agenda for any specific interview depended on the nature of the subject's own involvement with one or more of the issues. The interviews, when they worked best, became focused conversations about the individual's recollection of the debates that had attended the development of the policies in question. Sometimes the interviewee's own role in the policy process was a focus of discussion. In other instances, especially when an individual was on the losing side, it was the "politics of process," and the effects of this on the ultimate policy itself, which the respondent wanted to talk about. Always, we sought to confirm particular accounts of events with other participants, and to achieve a variety if not always a balance of perspectives.

American journalist and social historian Studs Terkel (1981) has suggested that most people have a story to tell, and that they usually like to be asked; we found this to be generally true. In a small minority of cases, the guardedness of the practised bureaucrat meant that individuals were less than forthcoming. In most cases, however, both volunteers and professionals were more than willing to talk about developments in Canadian sport that clearly mattered to them, whether they were part of these developments and therefore enthusiastic, or opposed them. In one sport, one of the investigators was privileged to sit in on a planning committee meeting, and thereby be privy to debate itself.

Interviews were conducted in Toronto and Kingston, as well as in Ottawa, where most took place. In a few cases, we conducted interviews on the telephone with people in the Maritimes or on the Prairies. Tape recorders were not used, but summaries of the interviews were made from notes immediately afterwards. The next stage of writing involved the preparation, from the interview records for each sport (seven to ten per sport), of an account of the policy-making process and the outstanding issues for each NSO. These formed the substance of our report to the Social Sciences and Humanities Research Council (Macintosh et al. 1987a) and other interested parties. The final stage involved identifying similarities and differences, and trying to relate these findings to our various theoretical frameworks. This is the process that produced a series of conference presentations and papers, feedback from other scholars interested in this topic, and, ultimately, this book.

Characteristics of National Professional Staff

In chapter 1, we alluded to the great growth in size and complexity of the NSOs in Ottawa during the 1970s and the early 1980s. We have also contended throughout the book that the full-time professional staff who were hired to fill these new positions in the NSOs have come to play an important and central role in the conduct of the day-to-day business of these organizations and in the taking of key policy decisions. These staff members bring to these tasks their own socio-cultural backgrounds and values as well as perspectives associated with their education and sport experience. Together, these influence the way they view the purpose and direction of their associations, as well as the manner in which they interact with volunteer members of national executives and national committees and with Sport Canada officials in the taking of policy decisions about key issues in sport. Thus, these demographic characteristics are central to any understanding and insights we may gain from our study of the policy-making process in NSOs.

In this appendix, we present some of the socio-economic and demographic characteristics of the professional staff in NSOs and Sport Canada consultants that we gathered in our questionnaire survey. Some 240 persons were sent questionnaires and 177 responded for a return rate of 74 per cent. Thirty-four per cent of the questionnaires sent out went to females; 31 per cent of the responses came from females. Respondents were divided into six categories according to job classification and the data about socio-economic and demographic characteristics were analysed according to gender and these six job categories. A full analysis of these data was presented in the *Canadian Journal of Sport Sciences* (Macintosh and Beamish 1988). Here we highlight some of the findings.

About two-thirds of the professional staff in our survey of Canada's high-performance sport delivery system were males, about 75 per cent of them were born in Canada, and about one-half had completed their high school education in Ontario. English was the mother tongue for about 80 per cent. Slightly more than one-half said they were bilingual; most of the rest spoke only English. These professional staff members were young, typically in their middle or late thirties. About 80 per cent of those surveyed possessed at least one university degree; of these, almost half also held a master's or higher-level degree. Of those that did not have a university degree, almost half had obtained a post-secondary diploma of some type. About one-half of the first university degrees earned were in physical education, recreation, and related fields. Over two-thirds of the rest of the first degrees were taken in arts and science. Second degrees earned were slightly more specialized; 35 per cent were in physical education, recreation, and related fields, 29 per cent in sport administration/business, and only 24 per cent in arts and science.

About one-quarter of the professional staff brought personal international-level sport experience to their jobs. Twenty-eight per cent had coached at the international level. These staff members had, on average, only six years of full-time employment experience in governmental and voluntary sport organizations. During this six-year period, the typical staff member had held, on average, two different positions in the sport bureaucracy. A surprising proportion (almost 40 per cent) came from low socio-economic backgrounds. An equal proportion, however, were from high socio-economic backgrounds.

The typical female was younger by about five and one-half years than her male counterpart and was even more likely to have been born in Canada, received her high school education in Ontario, and be anglophone. When compared to her male counterpart, she brought comparable educational experience to her job, but less often possessed national level or higher personal sport experience and, substantially less often, international-level coaching experience. Females had approximately one and a half fewer years of full-time sport employment experience and had a higher job turnover rate than did males. Women differed little from men in their socio-economic status background.

Only seven of the female respondents had been previously enrolled in one of the series of internship programs that have been offered since the early 1980s by the Fitness and Amateur Sport Women's Program for aspiring female sport professionals. The program itself, however, may have been at least partly responsible for the equal representation of females at the program coordinator level, where they occupied about 50 per cent of the jobs. In all other positions, females were underrepresented, typically holding about one-quarter of the positions. The matter of female representation in high-performance sport receives further attention in chapter 6.

It is against this background that we examine the sport policy-making process in the six selected NSOs and discuss the larger social and political issues which arise from policies taken by the NSOs and the federal government that have to do with high-performance sport.

Bibliography

Adelman, M., 1986. *A Sporting Time: New York City and the Rise of Modern Athletics*. Chicago: University of Illinois Press.

Anthony, D., 1980. *A Strategy for British Sport*. Kingston and Montreal: McGill-Queen's University Press.

Aronowitz, S., and H. Giroux, 1985. *Education Under Siege: The Conservative, Liberal, and Radical Debate over Schooling*. South Hadley, Mass.: Bergin and Garvey.

Axelrod, P., 1982. *Scholars and Dollars*. Toronto: University of Toronto Press.

Balbus, I., 1975. "Politics as sports: An interpretation of the political ascendancy of the sports metaphor in America." In L. Lindberg, ed., *Stress and Contradiction in Modern Capitalism*. Lexington, Ky.: D.C. Heath.

Banting, K., 1987. *The Welfare State and Canadian Federalism.* (second edition). Kingston and Montreal: McGill-Queen's University Press.

Beamish, R., 1978. "Socio-economic and demographic characteristics of the national executives of selected amateur sports in Canada (1975)." *Working Papers in the Sociological Study of Sports and Leisure*, 1(1):1–25. Kingston: Queen's University.

– 1982. "Some neglected political themes in sport study." Presented to the 77th Meeting of the American Sociological Association, San Francisco.

– 1985. "Sport executives and voluntary associations: A review of the literature and introduction to some theoretical issues." *Sociology of Sport Journal*, 2(3): 218–32.

Beamish, R., and J. Borowy, 1987. "High-performance athletes in Canada: From status to contract." In T. Slack and R. Hinings, eds., *The Organization and Administration of Sport*. London, Ont.: Sports Dynamics Publishers.

– 1988. *What Do You Do for a Living? I'm an Athlete*. Kingston, Ont.: Sport Research Group, Queen's University.

Beamish, R., and A. Johnson, 1987. "Socio-economic characteristics of Canada's current national team, high-performance athletes." Presented at the Annual Meeting of the North American Society for the Sociology of Sport, Edmonton, Alta.

Beer, S., 1983. *Designing Freedom*. CBC Massey Lectures, Toronto: CBC Publications.

Bell, D., 1976. *The Coming of the Post-Industrial Society*. New York: Basic Books.

Bella, L., 1987. *Parks for Profit*. Montreal: Harvest House.

Bellah, R., R. Madsen, W. Sullivan, A. Swidler, and S. Tipton, 1985. *Habits of the Heart: Individualism and Commitment in American Life*. Berkeley: University of California Press.

Bender, T., 1984. "The erosion of public culture: Cities, discourses, and professional disciplines." In T. Haskell, ed., *The Authority of Experts: Studies in History and Theory*. Bloomington: Indiana University Press.

Berger, P., B. Berger, and H. Kellner, 1974. *The Homeless Mind*. London: Penguin.

Berger, T., 1985. *Village Journey*. New York: Hill and Wang.

Berlin, I., 1969. *Four Essays on Liberty*. Oxford: Clarendon Press.

– 1972. *Fathers and Children*. Oxford: Clarendon Press.

Birrell, S., 1988. "Discourses on the gender/sport relationship: From women in sport to gender relations." In K. Pandolf, ed., *Exercise and Sport Science Reviews*, 16. New York: Macmillan.

Birrell, S., and D. Richter, 1987. "Is a diamond forever? Feminist transformations of sport." *Women's Studies International Forum*, 10(4): 395–409.

Bledstein, B., 1976. *The Culture of Professionalism: The Middle Class and the Development of Higher Education in America*. New York: Norton.

Bloom, A., 1987. *The Closing of the American Mind*. New York: Touchstone/ Simon and Schuster.

Boileau, R., 1982. "Role et statu du professionel de l'activite physique." In *L'Education Physique, Qu Va La Profession*. Montreal: Bellarmin-Desport.

Boileau, R., F. Landry, and Y. Trempe, 1976. "Les Canadiens Francais et les grands jeux internationaux." In R. Gruneau and J. Albinson, eds., *Canadian Sport: Sociological Perspectives*. Don Mills: Addison-Wesley.

Broom, E., and R. Baka, 1978. *Canadian Governments and Sport*. Ottawa: CAHPER *Sociology of Sport Monograph Series*.

Brown, J., 1986. "Professional language: Words that succeed." *Radical History Review*, 34(1):33–51.

Bryson, L., 1987. "Sport and the maintenance of masculine hegemony." *Women's Studies International Forum*, 10(4):349–60.

Bucher, R., and A. Strauss, 1961. "Professions in process." *American Journal of Sociology*, 66:325–34.

Campagnolo, I., 1977. *Toward a National Policy on Amateur Sport: A Working Paper*. Ottawa: Ministry of State, Fitness and Amateur Sport.

– 1979. *Partners in Pursuit of Excellence: A National Policy on Amateur Sport*. Ottawa: Ministry of State, Fitness and Amateur Sport.

Canada, 1969. *Report of the Task Force on Sport for Canadians*. Ottawa: Queen's Printer.

– 1987. *Census Canada 1986: Population and Dwelling Characteristics*. Ottawa: Census Divisions and Subdivisions, Quebec.

– 1988. *Toward 2000: Building Canada's Sport System*. Report of the Task Force on National Sport Policy. Ottawa: Fitness and Amateur Sport.

Cantelon, H., and R. Gruneau, eds., 1982. *Sport, Culture and the Modern State*. Toronto: University of Toronto Press.

Carr, W., and S. Kemmis, 1986. *Becoming Critical: Education, Knowledge, and Action Research*. Brighton and Philadelphia: Falmer Press.

Carrigan, T., R. Connell, and J. Lee, 1985. "Toward a new sociology of masculinity." *Theory and Society*, 14(5):551–604.

Carrington, B., and O. Leaman, 1985. "Athleticism and the reproduction of gender and ethnic marginality." *Leisure Studies*, 4(2):205–17.

Castells, M., 1977. *The Urban Question*. London: Edward Arnold.

Coalter, F., J. Long, and B. Duffield, 1986. *Rationale for Public Sector Investment in Leisure*. London: Sports Council and Economic and Social Research Council.

Coe, S., 1985. *Olympic Review: Preparing for 1988*. London: Sports Council.

Collins, R., 1978. *The Credential Society: An Historical Sociology of Education and Stratification*. Berkeley: University of California Press.

Connell, R., 1983. *Which Way Is Up? Essays in Class, Sex, and Culture*. Sydney: Allen and Unwin.

– 1987. *Gender and Power*. Stanford: Stanford University Press.

Courchene. T., 1978. "Avenues of adjustment: The transfer system and regional disparities." In M. Walker, ed., *Canadian Confederation at the Crossroads*. Vancouver: Fraser Institute.

Craib, I., 1987. "Masculinity and male dominance." *Sociological Review*, 35(4):721–43.

Critcher, C., 1986. "Radical theorists of sport: The state of play." *Sociology of Sport Journal*, 3(4):333–43.

Crozier, M., S. Huntington, and J. Watanuki, 1976. *The Crisis of Democracy*. New York: Trilateral Commission.

Cullen, J., 1983. "An occupational taxonomy by professional characteristics: Implications for research." *Journal of Vocational Behaviour*, 22(3):257–67.

Deem, R., 1987. "The politics of women's leisure." *Sociological Review*, Monograph 33:210–28.

Demers, P., 1988. "University training of physical educators." In J. Harvey and H. Cantelon, eds., *Not Just a Game*. Ottawa: University of Ottawa Press.

Dingwall, R., 1976. "Accomplishing profession." *Sociological Review*, 24: 331–49.

Drucker, P., 1974. *Management: Tasks, Responsibilities, Practices*. New York: Harper and Row.

Dunleavy, P., 1980. *Urban Political Analysis*. London: Macmillan.

Edelman, M., 1977. *Political Language: Words That Succeed and Policies That Fail*. New York: Academic Press.

Ferguson, K., 1984. *The Feminist Case against Bureaucracy*. Philadelphia: Temple University Press.

Fine, G., 1987. *With the Boys*. Chicago: University of Chicago Press.

Fitness and Amateur Sport, 1982. *Women in Sport Leadership: Summary of National Survey*. Ottawa.

– 1984. *Drug Use and Doping Control in Sport – A Sport Canada Policy*. Ottawa.

– 1985. *Women in Sport Leadership: Summary of National Survey*. Ottawa.

– 1986a. *Sport Canada Policy on Women in Sport*. Ottawa: Minister of Supply and Services.

– 1986b. *Annual Report*. Ottawa: Minister of Supply and Services.

– 1988. *Quadrennial Planning and Evaluation Guide, 1988–92*. Ottawa.

Fletcher, S., 1984. *Women First: The Female Tradition in English Physical Education: 1880–1980*. London: Athlone Press.

Forester, J., 1985. "Critical theory and planning practice." In J. Forester, ed., *Critical Theory and Public Life*. Cambridge, Mass.: MIT Press.

Foucault, M., 1980. *Power/Knowledge*. Brighton: Harvester Press.

Friedan, B., 1988. "An evening with the author of the Feminine Mystique." A public address at the University of California, Santa Barbara.

Freidson, E., 1970. *Professional Dominance: The Social Structure of Medical Care*. New York: Atherton.

– 1984. "Are professions necessary?" In T. Haskell, ed., *The Authority of Experts: Studies in History and Theory*. Bloomington: Indiana University Press.

Garson, B., 1988. *The Electronic Sweatshop: How Computers Are Transforming the Office of the Future into the Factory of the Past*. New York: Simon and Schuster.

Geison, G., ed., 1983. *Professions and Professional Ideologies in America*. Chapel Hill: University of North Carolina Press.

Giddens, A., 1979. *Central Problems in Social Theory*. London: Macmillan.

– 1982. *Profiles and Critiques in Social Theory*. London: Macmillan.

– 1984. *The Constitution of Society*. London: Polity Press.

Gilligan, C., 1982. *In a Different Voice*. Cambridge, Mass.: Harvard University Press.

Globe and Mail, 3 October 1988. "Golden efforts save Canada's battered pride." Toronto: C5.

– 29 March 1989. "Soviet sport authority punished 290 for drug infractions, report reveals." Toronto: A1.

Goldlust, J., 1987. *Playing for Keeps: Sport, the Media, and Society*. Melbourne: Longman Cheshire.

Goodale, T., 1985. "Prevailing winds and bending mandates." In T. Goodale and P. Witt, eds., *Recreation and Leisure: Issues in an Era of Change*. State College, Penn.: Venture Publishing.

Goodhart, P., and C. Chataway, 1968. *War without Weapons*. London: W.H. Allen.

Gouldner, A., 1979. *The Future of Intellectuals and the Rise of the New Class*. New York: Oxford University Press.

Gratton, C., 1988. "The production of Olympic champions: International comparisons." Presented at Leisure Studies Association, Second International Conference, Brighton.

Gruneau, R., 1976. "Class or Mass: Notes on the democratization of Canadian amateur sport." In R. Gruneau and J. Albinson, eds., *Canadian Sport: Sociological Perspectives*. Don Mills: Addison-Wesley.

– 1983. *Class, Sports and Social Development*. Amherst: University of Massachusetts Press.

– 1984. "Leisure, freedom and the state." In A. Tomlinson, ed., *Leisure: Politics, Planning and People*, Vol. 1. London: Leisure Studies Association.

– 1988. "Modernization or hegemony: Two views on sport and social development." In J. Harvey and H. Cantelon, eds., *Not Just a Game*. Ottawa: University of Ottawa Press.

– 1989. "Making spectacle: A case study in television sports production." In L. Wenner, ed., *Media, Sports and Society*. Beverly Hills: Sage Publications (in press).

Gruneau, R., and H. Cantelon, 1987. "Capitalism, commercialism and the Olympics." In J. Segrave and D. Chu, eds., *The Olympic Games in Transition*. Urbana, Ill.: Human Kinetics Press.

Guay, D., 1981. *L'Histoire de l'Education Physique au Quebec: Conceptions et Evenements (1830–1980)*. Chicoutimi, Que.: Gaetan Morin.

Guttmann, A., 1978. *From Ritual to Record*. New York: Columbia University Press.

Habermas, J., 1971. *Toward a Rational Society*. London: Heinemann.

– 1972. *Knowledge and Human Interests*. London: Heinemann.

Hall, M.A., 1987. "Masculinity as culture: The discourse of gender and sport." Presented at the Congress on Movement and Sport in Women's Life, Jyvaskala, Finland.

– 1989. "How should we theorize gender in the context of sport?" In M. Messner and D. Sabo, eds., *Critical Perspectives on Sport, Patriarchy and Men*. Champaign, Ill.: Human Kinetics Press (forthcoming).

Hall, M.A., D. Cullen, and T. Slack, 1989. "Organizational elites recreating themselves: The gender structure of national sport organizations." *Quest*, 41(1):28–45.

Hall, S., and M. Jacques, eds., 1983. *The Politics of Thatcherism*. London: Lawrence and Wishart.

Hallett, W., 1981. "A history of federal government in the development of sport in Canada: 1943–1979." Unpublished doctoral dissertation, University of Alberta.

Hardy, S., 1987. "Graduate curriculums in sport management: The need for a business orientation." *Quest*, 39:207–16.

Hargreaves, J., 1985. "From social democracy to authoritarian populism: State intervention in sport and physical education in contemporary Britain." *Leisure Studies*, 4(2):219–26.

– 1986. *Sport, Power and Culture*. Cambridge: Polity Press.

Harvey, J., 1983. *Le Corps Programme*. Montreal: Editions St Martin.

– 1988. "Sport policy and the welfare state: An outline of the Canadian case." *Sociology of Sport Journal*, 5(4):315–29.

Harvey, J., and R. Proulx, 1988. "Sport and the state in Canada." In J. Harvey and H. Cantelon, eds., *Not Just a Game*. Ottawa: University of Ottawa Press.

Haskell, T., ed., 1984. *The Authority of Experts: Studies in History and Theory*. Bloomington: Indiana University Press.

Hayek, F., 1960. *Constitution of Liberty*. London: Routledge/Kegan Paul.

Hearn, J., and P.W. Parkin, 1987. *"Sex" at "Work": The Power and Paradox of Organizational Sexuality*. Brighton: Wheatsheaf.

Hennig, M., and A. Jardim, 1977. *The Managerial Woman*. Garden City, New York: Anchor Press/Doubleday.

Hinings, R., and T. Slack, 1987. "The dynamics of quadrennial plan implementation in national sport organizations." In T. Slack and R. Hinings, eds., *The Organization and Administration of Sport*. London, Ont.: Sports Dynamics Publishers.

Hirsch, E., 1987. *Cultural Literacy*. New York: Houghton-Mifflin.

Hoberman, J., 1984. *Sport and Political Ideology*. London: Heinemann.

Hollands, R., and R.S. Gruneau, 1979. "Social class and voluntary action in the administration of Canadian amateur sport." *Working Papers in the Sociological Study of Sports and Leisure*, 2(3):1–40. Kingston: Queen's University.

House of Commons (HC), 1957. *Debates*. Ottawa.

Hudson, K., 1978. *The Jargon of the Professions*. London: Macmillan.

Hughes, E., 1958. *Men and Their Work*. Glencoe, Ill.: Free Press.

Hynes, M., 29 March 1989. "U.S. group disputes Francis claim." *Globe and Mail*. Toronto: A13–14.

– 7 May 1989. "Fraud explains lack of positive drug tests, inquiry told." *Globe and Mail*. Toronto: A1–2.

Ignatieff, M., 1986. *The Needs of Strangers*. London: Penguin.

Imray, L., and A. Middleton, 1983. "The public and the private: Marking the boundaries." In E. Gamarnikow et al., eds., *The Public and the Private*. London: Heinemann.

Ingham, A., 1975. "Occupational subcultures in the work world of sport." In D. Ball and J. Loy, eds., *Sport and Social Order*. Don Mills: Addison-Wesley.

– 1985. "From public issue to personal trouble: Well-being and the fiscal crisis of the state." *Sociology of Sport Journal*, 2(1):43–55.

Johnson, T., 1972. *Professions and Power*. London: Macmillan.

Johnston, R., and D. Robbins, 1977. "The development of specialties in industrialized science." *Sociological Review*, 25(1):87–108.

Kanter, R., 1977. *Men and Women of the Corporation*. New York: Basic Books.

Katz, M., 1982. "Critical literacy: A conception of education as a moral right and a social ideal." In R. Everhart, ed., *The Public School Monopoly*. Cambridge, Mass.: Ballinger.

Kemp, R., 1985. "Planning, public hearings, and the politics of discourse." In J. Forester, ed., *Critical Theory and Public Life*. Cambridge, Mass.: MIT Press.

Kenyon, G., 1977. "Factors influencing the attainment of elite status in track and field." In *Proceedings of the 1976 Post Olympic Games Symposium*. Ottawa: Coaching Association of Canada.

Kidd, B., 1980. "The Canadian state and sport: The dilemmas of intervention." Presented at the Annual Conference of the National Association for Physical Education in Higher Education, Brainerd, Minn.

– 1981. "Sport, dependency, and the Canadian state." *Momentum*, 5(2).

– 1987. "Sports and masculinity." In M. Kaufman, ed., *Beyond Patriarchy: Essays by Men*. Toronto: Oxford University Press.

– 1 October 1988. "What happened to amateur sport?" Special to *Globe and Mail*. Toronto: D1,D8.

Knoppers, A., 1987. "Gender and the coaching profession." *Quest*, 39:9–22.

Konrad, G., and I. Szelenyi, 1979. *The Intellectuals on the Road to Class Power*. New York: Harcourt Brace Jovanovich.

Lalonde, M., 1974. *A New Perspective on the Health of Canadians – A Working Document*. Ottawa: Department of National Health and Welfare.

Lapierre, L., ed., 1987. *If You Love This Country*. Toronto: McClelland and Stewart.

Larson, M., 1977. *The Rise of Professionalism: A Sociological Analysis*. Berkeley: University of California Press.

– 1984. "The production of expertise and the constitution of expert power." In T. Haskell, ed., *The Authority of Experts: Studies in History and Theory*. Bloomington: Indiana University Press.

Laurin, S., 1988. "The effects of government initiated planning systems on the structure of provincial sport organizations." Presented at the Sociology Colloquium, "New Directions in the Sociology of Amateur Sport in Canada," University of Calgary, Calgary.

Lawson, H., 1984. "Problem-setting for physical education and sport." *Quest*, 36(1):48–60.

– 1985. "Knowledge for work in the physical education profession." *Sociology of Sport Journal*, 2(1):9–24.

Lincoln, Y., and E. Guba, 1985. *Naturalistic Inquiry*. London and Beverley Hills: Sage.

Lynn, K., ed., 1965. *The Professions in America*. Boston: Houghton Mifflin.

Macintosh, D., 1986. "Physical education in higher education: A Canadian perspective." In *Trends and Developments in Physical Education*. London: E. and F.N. Spon.

– 1988. "The federal government and voluntary sports associations." In J. Harvey and H. Cantelon, eds., *Not Just a Game*. Ottawa: University of Ottawa Press.

Macintosh, D., and J. Albinson, 1985. "An evaluation of the Athlete Assistance Program." Report to Sport Canada. Kingston: Social Program Evaluation Group, Queen's University.

Macintosh, D., and R. Beamish, 1987. "Female advancement in national level sport administration positions." Presented at the ICHPER/CAHPER Conference, Vancouver, BC.

– 1988. "Socio-economic and demographic characteristics of national sports administrators." *Canadian Journal of Sport Sciences*, 13(1):66–72.

Macintosh, D., R. Beamish, D. Whitson, D. Greenhorn, and M. MacNeill, 1987a. "Professional staff and policy making in national sport organizations." A research report presented to the Social Sciences and Humanities Research Council of Canada. Kingston: Queen's University.

Macintosh, D., with T. Bedecki and C.E.S. Franks, 1987b. *Sport and Politics in Canada*. Kingston and Montreal: McGill-Queen's University Press.

MacIntyre, A., 1981. *After Virtue: A Study in Moral Theory*. South Bend, Ind.: University of Notre Dame Press.

MacKinnon, C., 1987. "Women, self-possession and sport." In *Feminism Unmodified: Discussions on Law and Life*. Cambridge: Harvard University Press.

Macpherson, C.B., 1973. *Democratic Theory: Essays in Retrieval*. Oxford: Clarendon Press.

— 1985. *The Rise and Fall of Economic Justice*. London: Oxford University Press.

Mangan, A.J., 1981. *Athleticism in the Victorian and Edwardian Public Schools*. Cambridge: Cambridge University Press.

Markus, M., 1987. "Women, success, and civil society: Submission to, or subversion of, the achievement principle." In S. Benhabib and D. Cornell, eds., *Feminism as Critique*. Minneapolis: University of Minnesota Press.

Martens, R., 1987. "Science, knowledge, and sport psychology." *Sport Psychologist*, 1(1):29–55.

Meisel, J., and V. Lemieux, 1972. "Ethnic relations in Canadian voluntary associations." *Documents of the Royal Commission on Bilingualism and Biculturalism*, 13. Ottawa: Information Canada.

Mercer, D., 1984. "Unmasking technocratic geography." In M. Billinge et al., eds., *Recollections of a Revolution*. London: Macmillan.

Milne, D., 1986. *Tug of War: Ottawa and the Provinces Under Trudeau and Mulroney*. Toronto: Lorimer.

Ministry of State, Fitness and Amateur Sport, 1985. *Sport Canada Contributions Program 1986–1987*. Ottawa.

Misgeld, D., 1985. "Education and cultural invasion: Critical social theory, education as instruction, and the 'Pedagogy of the Oppressed' ". In J. Forester, ed., *Critical Theory and Public Life*. Cambridge, Mass.: MIT Press.

Mishra, R., 1977. *Society and Social Policy*. London: Macmillan.

Morrison, M., R.P. White, and E. VanVelsor, 1987. *Breaking the Glass Ceiling*. Don Mills: Addison-Wesley.

Munro, J., 1970. *A Proposed Sports Policy for Canadians*. Ottawa: Department of National Health and Welfare.

Nelson, R., 1976. *The Illusions of Urban Man*. Ottawa: Ministry of State for Urban Affairs.

Nozick, R., 1974. *Anarchy, State and Utopia*. Oxford: Blackwell.

O'Connor, J., 1973. *The Fiscal Crisis of the State*. New York: St Martin's.

Offe, C., 1984. *Contradictions of The Welfare State*. London: Hutchison.

— 1985. *Disorganized Capitalism*. Cambridge: Polity Press.

Ontario, 1988. *A Provincial Policy for Women in Physical Activity and Sport*. Toronto: Ministry of Tourism and Recreation.

Ottawa Citizen, 3 Oct. 1988. "Blend of science, arts should be requirements for degree, academics say." Ottawa: A10.

Panitch, L., ed., 1977. *The Canadian State: Political Economy and Political Power*. Toronto: University of Toronto Press.

Parsons, T., 1954. "The professions and social structure." In *Essays in Sociological Theory*. New York: The Free Press.

— 1968. "Professions." In D. Sills, ed., *International Encyclopedia of the Social Sciences*. New York: Macmillan.

Rawls, J., 1971. *A Theory of Justice*. Oxford: Clarendon.

Regan, G., 1981. *A Challenge to the Nation: Fitness and Amateur Sport in the 80s*. Ottawa: Ministry of State, Fitness and Amateur Sport.

Roberts, K., 1978. *Contemporary Society and the Growth of Leisure*. London: Longmans.

Rorty, R., 1979. *Philosophy and the Mirror of Nature*. Princeton: Princeton University Press.

Rosenblum, K., 1986. "The conflict between and within genders: An appraisal of contemporary American femininity and masculinity." *Sociological Inquiry*, 56:93–104.

Roth, J., 1974. "Professionalism: The sociologist's decoy." *Sociology of Work and Occupations*, 1(1):6–23.

Saunders, P., 1984. *Social Theory and the Urban Question*. London: Hutchinson.

Schon, D., 1979. "Generative metaphor: A perspective on problem setting in social policy." In A. Ortony, ed., *Metaphor and Thought*. New York: Cambridge University Press.

Schrodt, B., 1984. "Federal programs of physical recreation and fitness: The contributions of Ian Eisenhardt and PRO-REC." *Canadian Journal of History of Sport*, 15(2):45–61.

Simpson, J., 1976. *Towards Cultural Democracy*. Strasbourg: Council of Europe.

Slack, T., 1985. "The bureaucratization of a voluntary sport organization." *International Review of Sport Sociology*, 20(3):145–66.

Slack, T., and R. Hinings, 1987a. "Planning and organizational change: A conceptual framework for the analysis of amateur sport organizations." *Canadian Journal of Sport Sciences*, 12(4):185–93.

— 1987b. "Changes in the provincial sport organizations; 1985–6." A report prepared for Alberta Recreation and Parks. Edmonton: University of Alberta.

Smith, D., 1987. *The Everyday World as Problematic: A Feminist Sociology*. Toronto: University of Toronto Press.

Sparks, R., 1985. "Knowledge structures in sport and physical education." *Sport Sociology Journal*, 2(1):1–8.

Sport Marketing Council, 1986. *Introduction to National Sport Governing Bodies*. Ottawa.

Sports Council, 1982. *Sport in the Community ... The Next Ten Years*. London: Sports Council.

Stacey, J., and B. Thorne, 1985. "The missing feminist revolution in sociology." *Social Problems*, 32(4):301–16.

Stake, R., 1980. "The case study method in social inquiry." In H. Simons, ed., *Toward a Science of the Singular*. Norwich: University of East Anglia.

Starr, P., 1982. *The Social Transformation of American Medicine*. New York: Basic Books.

Sullivan, W., 1986. *Reconstructing Public Philosophy*. Berkeley: University of California Press.

Taylor, P., 1988. "The production of sporting excellence in England: A mixed economy problem." Presented at the Leisure Studies Association, Second International Conference, Brighton, England.

Terkel, S., 1981. *Working*. New York: Avon Books.

Theberge, N., 1985. "Toward a feminist alternative to sport as a male preserve." *Quest*, 37(2):193–202.

– 1987. "A preliminary analysis of the careers of women coaches in Canada." In T. Slack and R. Hinings, eds., *The Organization and Administration of Sport*. London: Sports Dynamics Publishers.

– 1988. "Social control and women in sport." In J. Freeman, ed., *Women: A Feminist Perspective* (second edition). Palo Alto, Cal.: Mayfield.

Thibault, L., T. Slack, and R. Hinings, 1988. "Professionalism, structures, and systems: The impact of professional staff on voluntary sport organizations." Presented at the Sociology Colloquium, "New Directions in the Sociology of Amateur Sport in Canada," University of Calgary, Calgary.

Thompson, J., 1984. *Studies in the Theory of Ideology*. Cambridge: Cambridge University Press.

– 1987. "Language and ideology: A framework for analysis." *Sociological Review*, 35:516–36.

Touraine, A., 1974. *The Post-Industrial Society*. London: Wildwood House.

Ulrich, D., 1987. "The role of transformational leaders in changing sport arenas." In T. Slack and R. Hinings, eds., *The Organization and Administration of Sport*. London, Ont.: Sports Dynamics Press.

Van Til, J., 1985. "Voluntarism and social policy." *Social Policy*, 15(Spring): 28–31.

Veysey, L., 1975. "Who's a professional? Who cares?" *Reviews in American History*, 3:419–23.

Vollmer, H., and D. Mills, 1966. *Professionalization*. Englewood Cliffs, NJ: Prentice Hall.

Walzer, M., 1983. *Spheres of Justice*. New York: Harper Colophon.

West, J., 1973. *Fitness, Sport and the Canadian Government*. Ottawa: Fitness and Amateur Sport Branch.

Westland, C., 1979. *Fitness and Amateur Sport in Canada*. Ottawa: Canadian Parks and Recreation Association.

Whitson, D., 1976. "Method in sport sociology: The potential of a phenomenological contribution." *International Review of Sport Sociology*, 11(4):53–68.

– 1978. "Sociology, psychology and Canadian sport." *Canadian Journal of Applied Sport Science*, 3(2):71–8.

– 1984. "Sport and hegemony: On the construction of the dominant culture." *Sociology of Sport Journal*, 1(1):64–78.

– 1990. "The social construction of masculinity." In M. Messner and D. Sabo, eds., *Critical Perspectives on Sport, Patriarchy and Men*. Champaign, Ill.: Human Kinetics Press.

Wilensky, H., 1964. "The professionalization of everyone?" *American Journal of Sociology*, 70(2):137–48.

Williams, R., 1976. *Keywords*. London: Fontana.

Zeigler, E., 1983. "A proposal for the reunification of our professional and scholarly dimensions." *CAHPER Journal*, 50(2):17–19.

Zeller, S., 1988. *Inventing Canada: Early Victorian Science and the Idea of a Transcontinental Nation*. Toronto: University of Toronto Press.

Index